IN THE VAULT

FIGHTING THE BATTLE FOR YOUR HEART

Tolu Adesina

Foreword by Dr Sola Fola-Alade

A CIP catalogue record for this title is available from the British Library

Published by Random Wonders Press
London, UK
www.randomwonderspress.com

Printed in the United Kingdom.

I dedicate this book to the first person to encourage me to tell stories - my super hero. I miss you every day Daddy. I hope you're proud of me.

CONTENTS

FOREWORD

I remember like yesterday, the day when years ago Tolu walked into my ministry. My wife and I very quickly developed a fondness for this small but mighty and effervescent young lady, and now she has become a big sister to both my sons and a key part of our family. Today, I am extremely proud, not only of who she has become and to see how far she has come in God, but more so that I am holding a book she has written in my hands.

A few months ago, Tolu informed me she felt inspired by God to write a book, and within weeks she sent me the manuscript. Well, like they say, "the rest is history". The book in your hand is proof that she is a good student and her Father's (Pastor) Daughter. She has skillfully pulled together a myriad of nuggets from her growing years and walk with God by the tutelage of the Holy Spirit. She draws on her personal experiences and shares some of her mistakes, vulnerable moments and family experiences with openness, sincerity and candour. Tolu has not written an abstract or impractical book but one that derives from lessons learnt from her own personal journey. It is a book that highlights a path which almost every single lady will traverse and it helps to show the land mines to avoid and the way to navigate the path without falling prey to human and emotional predators of low self-esteem, self doubt and selling yourself cheap.

This book shows how precious you are in God's eyes. We all need to be valued but it all starts by knowing our real value in God and not deriving our value from people and things and this book will serve as a pivotal key into understanding and unlocking your true value. I believe this book will serve as a tool for healing emotional hurts and, with guidance from the Holy Spirit, help you begin your destiny journey. It will help sustain you as you walk daily with God until you arrive in eternity.

I encourage you to take time out to read this compelling book. Enjoy the read.

Dr. Sola Fola-Alade, Lead Pastor, The Liberty Church London

THROWBACK

I have a favourite childhood memory. It may sound strange, but it's the time I died. I was pronounced dead for a little over an hour. Not dying. Not in a coma. Dead.

As a child, in Lagos, Nigeria, I didn't eat much. My mum took me from doctor to doctor, but each visit ended the same way: with the doctor reassuring her that I was healthy (if small for my age) and that she should keep trying to get me to eat. At each mealtime, my parents would provide multiple options with the hopes that one of them would entice me, but nothing ever worked. On a few occasions, after several days of going without food, my dad would force-feed me. This was very traumatic for my mum to watch (my screams would reduce her to a blubbing mess) and she quickly put a stop to it. The only thing I seemed to want to eat at the time was the guava fruit. The guava is a little green tropical fruit with thin, hard, crunchy skin and a sour taste that almost stung when you bit into it. I loved guavas so much that I would eat them for breakfast, second breakfast, lunch, dinner and dessert.

My mum backed my obsession with the fruit. She was simply happy for me to eat something—anything. It didn't matter to her that a guava has a million tiny seeds that were too hard to chew and too many to spit out that I would usually swallow them. At least I was getting something in my stomach. As long as the doctors didn't think anything else was wrong with me, she was happy to watch and see if I might start requesting other fruits or vegetables.

The day I died started like any other. It was guava season, which meant that I was surviving almost purely on the fruit. That Saturday afternoon, I was on the balcony of our house with a friend of mine who had come from across the street to play. The houses on my street had one feature in common though they were built in all different shapes and sizes. On the top floor facing the street, there was a large balcony, which spanned the full length of the front structure. Ours had tiled floors and large doors that led either to the dining room or to the living room (depending on which door). From the balcony, you could see onto other people's balconies or front yards so our street always felt like it was buzzing with activity. From people talking to each other across the street from their balconies, to children playing games while keeping a watchful eye of the front gate, there was always activity. We had been running around, but after a little while my stomach had begun feeling weird, so I stopped playing and decided to sit down.

My parents were not home, and our carer thought that perhaps the pain was because I hadn't eaten so she rushed over with a bowl of my beloved guava. But at the sight of them, I simply turned away. This was the first signal to her that something was off. As the afternoon wore on and evening set in, I got quieter and quieter (apparently this is not a natural state for me – even at five!) so she got very worried and decided to put me to bed while waiting on my parents to return. When they got home a little while later, my dad came straight to the room to check on me. When he saw me, I was clearly in agony and burning up with fever. He and my mum bundled me into the car and drove straight to their friend's private hospital (their equivalent of going to the emergency room).

I still have vivid memories of that evening. I remember us getting to the hospital. My mum was very worried, while my dad calmly told me that the doctor would take care of me. Looking at his face, I was calm--until I saw the nurse with a massive needle in her hand coming for me. I started to scream and tried to run, but my dad held me and told me everything would be fine. He made me look into his eyes while we rubbed noses (our little ritual: it used to make me laugh because I could never maintain eye contact while rubbing noses). Finally, I was calm enough for the nurse to stab me with her needle. Next thing I knew, I was being prepped and rolled into surgery.

It turned out I had appendicitis—my appendix had ruptured. What happened next, I heard from my dad. It has become something like folklore in our local community.

The surgery was successful, and once it was finished, the doctor went to see my parents to let them know things had gone well and that there were no complications. They then relaxed as they waited for me to wake up. An hour passed, then two. The doctors checked on me and assured my parents that it wasn't unusual for it to take a little longer for some kids to wake up after the operation. After the third hour, the doctor was visibly distressed. This was when my dad realised that they were struggling to wake me up. My mum still remembers how afraid she was. She actually collapsed when the doctors told her they were struggling to revive me and that things didn't look good.

Hours passed, but despite all the doctor's efforts, there was no progress. Eventually they decided there was nothing else they could do. Early the next morning, the doctor pronounced me dead. But he couldn't have been prepared for what happened next. Apparently one of the nurses spoke too loudly and my dad overheard that his only daughter was dead.

Let me provide some context here. In Nigeria, during my childhood, death by medical negligence was very common. Often seemingly uncomplicated procedures ended in loss of life because a doctor or nurse forgot to perform some basic act. Add to that the fact that my parents had lost a child (my sister) years earlier, and you can see why my dad would be willing to do anything to ensure that the medical staff did not give up on me too soon.

In a country where you are your own electrical supply due to poor infrastructure and consistent power cuts, it was not unusual to find people driving around with several jerry-cans filled with diesel in their boot. People liked to be prepared and have enough stock for their generators, which they depended on to provide electrical power to their homes. On this day, my parents, having not had a chance to off-load the car before having to rush me to the hospital, had some diesel in the boot of their car. My dad went down after overhearing the nurse, got a can of diesel and started pouring it within the hospital grounds.

You have to remember that this was a small private hospital owned by a friend of my father's so it didn't take much effort to do this without scrutiny. My father then went back and let the doctor know that he was aware that they were going to stop trying to revive me. If that really was the case, he said, he had put plans in place to ensure no one would be leaving the building.

My dad was a jovial man. I have very few memories where my dad's dazzling smile did not make an appearance. But with one look, the doctor could see that my dad was not the usual friendly man he knew. He raised an alarm that could be heard on the street below, and people started gathering. But my dad was unwilling to back down. So, with the smell of diesel in their nostrils in a country with little to no fire service, the doctors and nurses got back to work trying to revive me. Talk about working under pressure!

An hour later, I finally stirred. No one can explain what changed or why it took so long. All they say is that I woke up and asked for a drink. The relief the doctor and nurses must have felt! More importantly, the joy my parents must have experienced knowing they wouldn't have to grieve over another child. For the rest of my dad's life, it was a struggle for anyone – even my mum – to separate us.

Thinking of this story always makes me smile. Maybe it's an odd story to open with, but it's one of my favourite memories. How many people can say that their father's love literally brought them back from the dead? I actually wrote that line while smiling from ear to ear, and while I am (mostly!) kidding, it's one of many memories I have where I was made to feel loved. Despite all that life has thrown at me since – from loss to rejection to shame to a broken heart and everything in between – this story reminds me that there are people to whom I matter. This memory is dear to me because it reminds me of a time when I was enough. A time when I was so loved, someone was willing to give his life for me. I didn't even have to do anything to earn that love: all I had to do was be me.

In my darkest moments, God has used this story to illustrate the love that is possible—the love of a father and the sacrifices he is willing to make in order that we can have life in full and in abundance. This makes me think of the scripture where it tells me of how God put his love on the line for me (and you) by offering his Son (read himself) in sacrificial death just to set me right in him so my life can expand and deepen in meaning (Romans 5:8-11). Isn't that the best thing you've ever heard?

Regardless of whether your natural father was present or not, the true ultimate father (God) says he loves you (and me) so much that the thought of us not living our best life and being in relationship with him isn't something he can stand. My dad couldn't bear the thought of not having me in his life; of not seeing me every day; of not talking to me and sharing his heart and mind with me; of not watching me grow into a woman he would be proud to call his daughter. He would rather die than deal with that pain. I believe that is only a small glimpse into how God sees us. All that my dad displayed in that hospital room pales in comparison to the passion with which God loves you and me. God sent his only son to die for us so we can have access to true love – a father's love.

When you look at the world around you, it can seem crazy that someone could love you that much. But my experience as a five-year-old shows that that kind of love is possible. I told that story so that we can share in that love together, as you explore this journey with me.

1

MY WORLD IN PIECES

Even in laughter the heart may ache…
Proverbs 14:13 NIV

"Can Tol-lu Ade-c-na please make her way to Mrs. Dixon's office immediately? Thank You."

I was in music class being generally mischievous as usual when I heard my name over the tannoy. It had never happened before. Since I had moved to London at the age of 12 to further my education, I had become known as being quite the prankster but I had a knack for not getting caught. On the very few occasions where my teachers had known it was me, I had been able to sweet talk my way out of the mess. So it was a shock to the entire class to hear my name called. My music teacher looked over at me and, seeing the look of dread plastered on my face, walked over and gave me the nudge I needed to get up and make the long walk upstairs to the headmistress' office. Mrs. Dixon was a rather petite, blond, older lady. We girls respected her. She was known to be fair, but very firm. Her office was not a place you wanted to be called to.

As I approached her office, I knew something was wrong. Normally, the two ladies at reception took your name and asked you to sit until you were called. But on this fateful day, Mrs. Dixon herself was my welcoming party. I was very intuitive as a child, and even though she smiled when she saw me, I immediately felt it—the cold feeling of impending doom creeping up my back.

"Don't worry, you're not in trouble," she told me. She must have read the worried look on my face as fear of a telling off.

We went into her office, and she asked me to have a seat. I was very uncomfortable and asked her what was wrong. She looked so sad, but that's when she said it. "I'm so sorry to have to tell you this but your father passed away this morning."

I still remember how cold I felt. I started saying "No" over and over. She rushed over to hold me as I fell off the chair. Why did he have to suffer? I asked her. She said something, but I didn't hear her. Her lips were moving but her words didn't reach me. I kept thinking of how hard I prayed the night before. I kept thinking of all the plans I had made for that evening after school, when I would see him and tell him all about my day. I was crying hysterically and asking her if he was at peace now. I kept asking, "Why did he leave me?" and then saying, "But he would never leave me." It was the hardest thing I have ever been through.

Typing these words, even now, have been extremely tough. I still struggle to this day to share all I felt, said or experienced that day and in the days that followed. For a while I shut down, and it was like my mind was blank and I had no memories. I just couldn't believe that it was true. It couldn't be. I just wanted my daddy.

"The company of many doesn't erase the absence of one"
Author Unknown

I was 14 and on that cold January day, time froze. Anger stirred in me that day which lasted for years. My emotions started to spiral out of control. I was angry at everyone and everything, but I was especially angry at God. I had only ever prayed to ask him for one thing. Only one. And He couldn't even do that.

My father was an amazing man. It was only after his death that we got a glimpse into how much care he showed others and how many lives he touched - all in silence. He had put whole families through school, paid people's rent, and mentored many at how to succeed in business. My mum still remembers her surprise as these people turned up at the house crying and lamenting, as if they couldn't imagine life without him. But for me, he was amazing in the simplest of ways. He loved me with his entire being and he made sure I knew it. My love for architecture comes from him. He would pick me up from school every day and take me to different sites (he was an engineer) and get me to imagine grand buildings before showing me the blueprints. Then we would return months later as the building was being constructed for him to teach me yet another life lesson. When I mentioned I wanted to get into people's heads, he automatically thought I meant I wanted to go into medicine, so he went out and bought land and we started designing my hospital. He didn't take me lightly. Every thought was explored and every feeling analysed in love. He was so funny and you could always find us whispering and laughing together. He loved to read, so he would get me to read books and then relate the story back to him. I would always add some drama to the retelling, and that's how I got into story telling.

He would push me in my academics and though I was bright, I was also lazy. I would rather play or tell stories than read my schoolbooks, so he sat with me every day to ensure I didn't rush through my homework. Afterwards, we would discuss current affairs and trends and then end with our nightly stories. He told the best stories.

Even when he told me off, he would reason with me. Sometimes I wished he would just smack me like my friends' parents did, but he wouldn't and wouldn't tolerate others doing so either. If it was something I said (I had a big mouth even then) he would tell me "This is not the Adesina way. We don't just spread our business. We talk to each other not everyone else." He was very big on discretion so he trained me early to be discreet with my words. He was truly my person. He just got me and he was the one I told everything to.

The shock of his death and the pain of his absence is something I don't discuss. Ever. It's been years and I still get a tightening in my chest when I think of my father. I always think of what he would say if he saw me now. No one can be harder on me than I am on myself because deep inside me I am always striving to be someone he would be proud of. I pick apart my words, my thoughts and my actions constantly because I know what is or isn't "the Adesina way." I fail often because I have been changed by the events experienced but I am always striving. I often go back to apologise to my mum after yet another outburst and to explain myself because that's how he trained me to be. He told me you should always explain yourself and listen to others' point of view. You don't have to agree, but you do have to let them express their truth.

One key fact about my dad was his faith in God. He loved God and was a minister in our local church. He was quite troublesome because he believed that faith and reason should not be mutually exclusive and used every avenue to get people to think through the scriptures and make Christianity practical.

So it was no surprise then that when he got sick, my response was to pray. He had taught me that God answers prayers – especially those of children. When he fell ill, and the doctors could not say what was wrong, he would respond with faith that God had a plan.

The night before he passed away, I was in the hospital with him as usual. There was a flurry of activity and I could see from my mum's face that something was really wrong. I remember he was still speaking to me as normal and it was only years later that my mum would tell me that at that point, I was the only one he recognised.

I hate seeing my mum upset, so I left the ward and went outside to sit on the bench close to the hospital entrance. That's when I decided to pray and bargain with God. I prayed till I felt he heard me and would heal my dad. I couldn't stand seeing my dad in pain. When he died and it seemed my prayers had been in vain, the rage I felt towards God can't be expressed. I hated Him with a passion. I became militant at disproving his existence. If I couldn't disprove it, then I tried to prove He was not a good God worthy of following.

"Pain is inevitable. Suffering is optional"
Haruki Murakami

My world had shattered, and I no longer knew where I fit in. The only constant was my anger. As the years went on, I learned to put a good face on, but my anger was never far from the surface. I didn't want to hear anything about God or his grace or his love. Living with pain or trauma or any such baggage takes its toll on you and it is unforgivingly relentless in its consistency. Most of that time is a blur for me. What I do remember is that I truly struggled to understand the love of God or God as a father through these times.

In my attempts to disprove the concept of a loving God, I ended up in church. That sounds really strange but I had exhausted myself in my quest to understand and find a place for my anger and many questions in my search for identity and love.   I had studied philosophy and theology in school/college in a bid to use logic to disprove the existence of a higher being and creator. This led me to being aware that there was so much science and logic couldn't explain but I needed to be convinced as to the essence of this, and in my exploring of different ideas and religious beliefs and tenets, I somehow came back full circle to the existence of a loving Jesus. There were no angelic encounters or voices from the sky – just an ache to make sense of my reality using reason and logic. This didn't happen overnight but was a gradual process and though, at first, I struggled to accept this Jesus had any bearing on my day to day life, I could acknowledge his existence as a historical figure but I wasn't interested in any form of relationship as all I was looking for was love in the here and now – the kind that lasted and never left me. I searched for it in the different relationships I had but it was always fleeting with parts of me left even more broken after the encounter.

Over the years, God has brought many people my way to show me His love. Though I didn't recognise them as agents of God's love then, I see now that I was protected in ways that could only be divine. Looking at where I am now to where I was, it wasn't by my will alone that I am here today. Mix my mother's prayers with the amazing people I met along the way, and we can see that God really doesn't give up on us even when we give up on him.

I battled really dark moments and have been mistreated by people that should have loved me, but I was still somehow shielded. I look back now and I know that my tenacity and stubbornness were also my saving grace. There were so many people and so many relationships I tried to sabotage simply because I couldn't see God in my pain.

My spiritual father Dr. Sola Fola-Alade (PSFA) is one of the key ways God reclaimed me back to Him. It was his church that I stumbled upon armed with my many questions and arguments. My pain and trauma started with the loss of my natural father and it took God placing me in the hands of my spiritual father for me to start the long walk home. I don't let people in often because I am afraid of what they would find under my smiley exterior but in PSFA and his family, I found acceptance and space to start working through my baggage. God really is relentless in his desire for a relationship with us. I still don't know how I found my way into PSFA's church, or how his beautiful wife, PBFA, opened her arms and heart to me so willingly, but through them and the amazing people I have since met through their ministry, God started me on a journey of restitution and love.

2

DISCONNECTED

Adversity is the diamond dust Heaven polishes its jewel with
Thomas Carlyle

I got my first job at the age of 16 at one of the major supermarket chains in the UK. It was one of my favourite times from my teens. I had never had any independence financially, but here I was, making my own money and able to (for the most part) decide how I wanted to spend it.

The shop was close to a top football club's grounds, so it was always busy – particularly on game day. Most people who worked in the store were young. Only two managers

15

were over 21, and everyone else was between 16 and 20. It was the first time I got to mix with all sorts of personalities from all over London. It was a blast. We were like a little family or club, and most times we did more talking than working. I was initially put on the shop floor to stack shelves but within a week, I was moved to the tills because I spent all my time talking and meeting people rather than stacking shelves. I was also, it turns out, a distraction for the boys: they would leave their aisles to come and stack my shelves while I just talked.

This was my first real exposure to boys. I had gone to an all-girls secondary school and had just made the decision to stay on for sixth form. The sixth form was technically mixed, but in fact there were only six boys in my year. Yes, you read that right. In a school of hundreds of girls, there were only six boys. Safe to say that my exposure on a day-to-day basis with the opposite sex was extremely limited.

I still remember my first day at work. I was so excited and felt so grown up. As I walked up the stairs towards the office to pick up my staff card, there was a young man walking down the stairs. He saw me and did a double take. I wasn't used to that. He literally froze on the stairs and stared at me until I was out of sight.

He would later become my first official boyfriend and he chased me for three years before I finally say yes. By chased, I mean persistent, constant love notes, songs and standing outside of my school gates in the freezing cold only for me to ignore him as he ran after me to give me yet another song he had written about me. He was nearly two years older than I was and he was a semi-pro footballer who was marked for stardom. He had his own apartment and made his own money driving a very nice car. But I wasn't interested. You see – the first time I saw him, his pants were sagging and I had this warped view that "good guys" don't sag their jeans. As I settled into my role in the shop and interacted with different people, he became more introverted and was very quiet around me barely saying a word.

So, I "dated" his friend. I was 16 so dating to me then was to enjoy the attention and as I wasn't allowed to have a boyfriend and had a strict schedule, sneak in moments where he could walk me home from school or work and maybe a cheeky kiss in the alleyway just before the house. "Dating" his friend lasted for 2 months and ended when he left the shop and moved away from the area. He, on the other hand, persisted regardless and though I was often mean to him and my friends would laugh at him, to him I was it! The funniest part was that I genuinely wanted him to leave me alone and one day, I finally told him and he heard me. So we decided to be friends. When we finally started dating, it happened purely by accident.

"Some walks you have to take alone"

S. Collins

I mentioned he was a semi-pro footballer. What I didn't mention is that there were several teams, both local and foreign, that were seriously looking to sign him. He was in training but getting paid to showcase with some teams while he and his agent decided on the next step. That meant that he was always working (Saturday matches) or training (Monday to Friday). I worked very close to his flat but lived about an hour and a half away by bus. On days when I worked, I would finish late, as you didn't leave till the shop closed which was often 9pm sometimes 9:30pm. In an effort to help me out, he would pick me up from work and drop me home (only 35 minutes by car). This was very convenient as I didn't want to be stuck on a bus in the cold of winter and he didn't mind the journey. His training finished later than the shop closing time so he went one step further and gave me his spare keys so I could walk to his flat and rest till he came back from training and could then take me home. This routine suited me as I was often exhausted (I stood for several hours at my job) and he would come back with food or would cook yummy meals before driving me home.

I had gotten very fond of him as well because once we agreed to be friends, he was no longer on edge with me and we would often talk for long hours about any and everything. I became his sounding board (his father left when he was young so he felt financially responsible for his mum and younger brother) and he was my support system as I decided what I wanted to study and where. I was a little older at this stage and getting ready for university (he didn't attend university as he had been playing football) so I felt and acted a little more mature!

He was handsome and tall and a footballer so with that came "fans" – tons of girls knew him (and he knew a few too!) but I never cared as I was just his friend – someone to tell him off when yet another girl turned up looking for him and disturbed my sleep as I waited for him in his flat. We would always laugh about it especially as some of the girls were "obsessed" with him over what he had and would offer him all sorts to get him to pay them attention yet he was uninterested in a relationship and would tell them that from the start.

Yet I was never threatened. I had no reason to be so confident (I was skinny with a big stomach, I spoke too fast, I laughed really loudly ALL the time – the list goes on) but I knew he still liked me and he hoped we would one day get together but he was willing to play the long game till I was ready – whatever that meant. He always made me feel like I was a gem he had found and he could not stop wanting it.

This was strangely intoxicating and was the start of me looking for my value and worth in how desirable a man found me. Here I was, having lost my dad – my person – at a young age, being exposed to being desired by a man just for who I was and not what I could offer him. He filled a gap for me I didn't realise I was craving. When I said yes to dating him, it was purely because I felt we were connected on a deeper level and I had finally found a love that would not leave me.

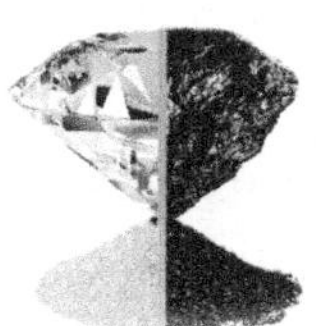

"No one told me that grief felt so like fear"
C.S Lewis

Imagine then, the depth of despair I felt when, after years of friendship, and a few months of dating, one night after I opened up to him and completely let go, he turns around to me and says he's waiting on an offer from a German team and if he gets it, he would be moving without notice. He said it light-heartedly but for a girl whose heart is as fragile as mine it felt like a slap in the face. Following the death of my father, I had struggled to make real emotional connections with people and he had become an escape from the constant ache inside me. That is probably why the news hit me the way it did. Instantly, I reverted back to the 14-year-old girl who had to say goodbye when she didn't want to. I immediately got up and starting packing up my things. He tried to stop me and back pedal but it was too late. If he intended to leave me at some point, why wait till then? Let's just end it now. He thought I was just being dramatic but that was it for me. I simply stopped picking up his calls and the relationship ended then.

I didn't realise it until years later, but a pattern had started to develop. I started walking into every encounter expecting that the person would leave me. I started thinking of myself as the kind of person that you wouldn't pick to have a lasting connection with. I was broken so that encounter deeply affected me. This pattern shaped my interactions for years to come.

As I grew older, started dating and interacting with the men that came my way, this pattern of thinking only solidified and before I knew it, I was fighting an inner battle between hoping for meaningful and lasting connections (finding my person) and anticipation of their exit. I have a lot of love to give but the sense of loss was never far away. This only served to add to my already fractured view of love and my growing lack of belief in my ability to be loved.

3

VANTAGE POINT

Sometimes you will never know the value of a thing until it becomes a memory
Dr. Seuss

There have been countless times that I have felt the sting of rejection from men that I had placed high hopes on. A hope of a lasting romance based on the intoxication of meeting and connecting with someone who seemed to be on the same page, is attractive (and tall), and has all the little elements necessary for a good and happy life together. Each time it ended, the pain of separation would hit me like a truck running through a brick wall and I would swear I would never let myself be blindsided or hurt like that again.

I'll give one episode as an example. I had travelled out of my hometown to go visit some friends in a different city. I needed a break from my regular routine and this seemed like a good way to de-stress. As soon as I was there, I started organising my itinerary and contacting the people I wanted to see. One of them is my close friend (Sujs) who, other than being like a sister, is also one of the most gracious hostesses I know. She always has an open house and loves to entertain. Knowing I was going to be around for only a few days, she made plans that Sunday to host me and a few of our other friends. That way, I got to spend time with most of my friends without the hassle of trying to plan individual lunch/dinner dates or travel from place to place. See why I love me some Sujs?

Now, as the dinner was on a Sunday afternoon and the guest list only featured my close friends, I was quite casual about the whole affair. I was looking forward to (over) eating loads of good food, having lively conversations, and laughing until my wig fell off.

On this day then, right after eating my third plate of the African deliciousness that is jollof rice, grilled meat and extra portion of gizdo, I had just managed to roll myself onto the sofa (barely) when her doorbell rings. I looked up at Sujs curiously as she walked to open the door (most of the party guests and their partners were already in the room and in the same food coma I was). When the door opened, in walked a stranger—one tall drink of water. I nearly choked.

Let me rewind a step. You see, my food coma was preceded by the pushing back of my wig, the unbuckling of my belt and a general nonchalance to my physical state. Here I was though, staring at this tall drink of water and feeling very parched, yet also looking a complete and utter mess. I tried willing the strength from my bulging stomach to move to my suddenly weak legs so I could do something – anything – to try and gather myself. Instead, everything seemed to be moving in slow motion and to make things worse, this fine specimen seemed to be saying something in my general direction. Stumbling over my words and struggling to roll over to my side so I could stand and rush out of the room, I managed to, unintelligibly, say hello before he walked over and sat himself right – next – to me! I'm pretty sure everything faded to black at that point.

Finding an excuse, I rushed to the bathroom to at least make sure my hair was on right. I tried to casually walk back to my seat and act unbothered, but I was suddenly hot and sweating harder than a woman in the throes of night fever. Forget that the air conditioner was on full blast, I was so hot I wanted to strip out of my clothes. But for decency's sake, I simply sat down and made a decision not to draw any more attention to myself. As Sujs helped him settle and fixed him a plate, I got some much needed respite from his hot stare to get my bestie Lollipop's attention and help in composing myself and coming up with a game plan to redeem the situation.

I'm still not sure how he didn't see the mess I was on that day, but he later told me that all he remembered about our first meeting was my smile. You can be sure I didn't say anything to contradict his version of events. Who am I to spoil what God is building by reminding him of my true state that day? When he finished eating, he came back and sat next to me and proceeded to engage me in conversation. Even though English is my first language, I truly struggled to speak or understand it that day. I must have looked like a bumbling fool to my friends, but somehow he found me endearing and kept looking for ways to talk to me one-on-one.

Finally, I relaxed. He was interesting, funny and very sweet – a complete gentleman. When he found out I was only visiting and was leaving a few days after, he asked when I would be returning so he could take me on a food tour (I thoroughly enjoy any activity that involves food). I was sold!

At the end of the evening, when it was just Sujs, Lollipop, TM (Lollipop's hubby) and I left in the house, I finally got the low-down on him. Turns out he was a friend of a friend and Sujs hadn't gotten any prior warning that he would be coming over. Lollipop was excited at the prospect of a love connection because he was a well-known and extremely successful businessman who was of a marriageable age (her words). She was already planning the speech she would give at our wedding. TM, being the cool, laid back guy he is, was more impressed by the wealth of general knowledge he displayed and how he composed himself during their conversation. I, on the other hand, was completely mute and in a state of shock. Did all that really just happen? Did I just spend the last three-and-a-half hours talking to this sexy human? Here I was, minding my business, when this guy makes an appearance and totally discombulates my whole existence.

Then they told me who he was and all my excitement leaked out of me like air from a balloon. I am pretty out-of-touch with the who's who in high society, so I can be forgiven for not realising who I had been talking to. You see, I had had enough experience on this journey of love by this time to know what I can or cannot handle in relationships. I don't like drama and I don't like to share. He was a well-known socialite who happens to be very successful at what he does. To me, this smelled like a recipe for disaster and the likelihood of dealing with "fans" – none of which I had the stomach for. TM reminded me that just a few minutes prior, I had been going on about how humble and sweet he seemed. It was a tough call—we lived in different cities, he's a famous name, and I am just a simple girl with no appetite for emotional stress. But finally, I decided to see what would happen.

When he called, we talked and laughed and made plans – it seemed I was wrong to have judged him. He seemed to be looking for the same thing I was and wasn't interested in games. My birthday was coming up, and he asked if I minded him flying in the night before, so he could be a part of the festivities my friends had planned. I was so touched. I had planned to hold myself back as I got to know him, but this thoughtful gesture melted me. I don't need much to make me happy, but thoughtfulness in anyone is my Achilles heel. So I allowed myself to get a little more relaxed and allowed him in a little further.

"You are a diamond dear: They can't break you"

Megan Hess

Three days before my birthday things suddenly got weird. Conversation, which had always flowed easily, suddenly got stilted. Two days before, he stopped responding to my calls or messages. At first, I thought it was due to his travel schedule, but on the day of my birthday, I heard nothing until late that evening when I got a happy birthday text. That was it. It was like I had imagined the whole scenario up to that point. I couldn't believe it. Was I not the same girl who had sworn I would not be blindsided by yet another guy who only seemed sweet?

I didn't even get mad – I just went numb. I ran deep into my shell in an attempt to deal with the anger and humiliation. From his continual silence, I deduced that I wasn't even worth an explanation. I had thought he was good guy: ambitious, driven, and single to boot. After all of the men who have used my heart as fodder, I thought that surely this was where I got my happy ending.

In my mind, I replayed every conversation. I didn't ask him to come down for my birthday – he offered. Maybe I should have refused? Maybe I should have been more appreciative? Perhaps he got bored? Was I too available? Should I have been more standoffish? I figured whatever I had done to put him off I could somehow fix. I went to war with myself, taking every inch of myself apart in an attempt to understand what I did wrong. But not once did I think it might have all been him. In moments of anger, I would think he was the devil's spawn, but then I would turn right around and think "I should have been nicer – I'm sure other girls are nicer." Looking back now, I genuinely don't know why I was so hung up on him or why I beat myself up so badly.

Truth is I didn't know if he was so amazing. I didn't really know him despite the conversations. He had shown me what he wanted me to see but he couldn't be that great if he could go ghost like that with no explanation (none I find acceptable anyway). But at the time I couldn't see it.

As chance would have it, a couple of years later, we bumped into each other (he was still interested – I was not) and he explained what had happened and why he had been such a waste-man (his words). I learned that what I thought had been an issue with me, had actually been all him. He met a beautiful, intelligent, witty, sweet woman (my words) and thought he had the capacity and bandwidth to handle the process of getting to know her with the intent of having her in his life long-term. Instead, what he found was a deficiency somewhere in him that all his wealth and status had previously covered up but my focus and drive exposed. So he bolted. What I thought was an issue of me not being good enough, not being pretty enough, not having much to offer someone of his status was actually not about me at all.

I learnt a very valuable lesson that has driven my interactions ever since. It took me years to accept this, but when people come around me and then choose to leave, it's not always about me. Often, it's about them and what they are dealing with.

Having that vantage point has been freeing and has allowed me to truly appreciate David's words in Psalm 84:11 – God will not withhold any good thing from me as his daughter. This perspective sometimes takes years to cultivate as the reality around you might look so different but you have to trust his word when he says He longs to bestow favour and honour on you. I have had to learn to go from internalising every departure as some sort of failure to understanding that if a guy walks away from me, that only means he was not the guy for me. The sense of loss I feel needs to be tempered with the belief that I am meant to love and be loved. He was only there to signboard the qualities I need and should value when I truly meet the right one. That person will know what he wants and be in a position to handle all the goodness I have to offer. Now, that is a vantage point I'm OK with.

4

DUMPED FOR MY HUE

She made herself stronger by fighting with the wind
Frances Hodgson Burnett

I never thought of myself as dark-skinned or light-skinned. Maybe that's because my parents never put emphasis on it, or maybe because when I was young no one ever commented on my skin tone in a derogatory way. I might think of myself as cute, hot or pretty, but my complexion was never a factor.

Don't get me wrong – I am very aware of the different sentiments some have about "pretty being light-skinned" or "mixed race [read: light-skinned] girls being the ultimate." It just had never affected my reality, and therefore never taken residence in my psyche.

So then imagine my shock and utter horror when, sitting across the table from a man I thought was a hottie, I was made to feel completely and utterly rejected because of my skin tone. He told me he liked me enough to be friends, but his type is "light-skinned." I was so shocked at first that I didn't even understand what he meant until later. Did he really imply that the only thing missing for him was the tone of my skin? I have heard a lot of reasons for not pursuing a relationship but this was new. It made no sense to me.

My mum is lighter-skinned than I am and so is my brother, but I didn't grow up in a home where the shade of your skin was a factor. Instead, what I do remember strongly from my childhood is that my mum had (and still does) very nice skin and would often get complimented wherever we went on her skin. Her skin was flawless. I don't think I've ever seen my mum with a pimple or anything that could mark her skin. Growing up, my mum did not wear makeup or jewellery. This served to further highlight her very beautiful skin. My dad would often comment on how beautiful she was in the presence of anyone who would listen and add, as an appendage, that she didn't need to wear makeup (I believe that was always directed at me to help me see I didn't need it).

You see my dad would often whisper complements to my mum and then in his next breath, whisper to me that I was like her and I was beautiful and so is my skin. It sounds odd, but I look more like my mum than my dad but I didn't like when people said this as I wanted to look like my dark-skinned, handsome, super intelligent, sweet, funny and always laughing super-hero (read: Dad). It was quite key that he would link us together because I was so enamored with my dad that I only saw him. He was everything to me and his opinion on anything was law. Him telling me I shouldn't wear makeup but I should instead be like my mum and concentrate on keeping my skin fresh and clear meant everything to me. I didn't wear makeup till my late teens/early 20s for this very reason. I still believe strongly in taking care of your skin, as that's the canvas on which makeup is applied to enhance the beauty that is already there. Her skin tone, however, was not something I heard mentioned or dwelt on so you can understand why I grew up valuing the quality of my skin rather than the shade of it.

"Beauty is to realise how full of love you are. Sensuality is to let some of that love shine through your body"
Nityananda Das

I remember at the age of 13 or thereabouts, finally starting to feel the stirs of my femininity. Before that, I was fully a tomboy who spent more time watching "Teenage mutant ninja turtles" (I even had the whole duvet set), reading and playacting with my dad and annoying my older brother by following him to all his football matches where I would attempt to play (with or without my shoes on!). Makeup, dresses and dolls were not on my radar. In fact, when I was much younger and before I moved to the UK, my mum's best friend would often come to Lagos from London to visit us over the summer (the families visited each other in alternate yearly cycles) and her twin daughters would come with their many dolls. I would always ignore them at doll playing times (which often coincided with my reading time) or break the dolls if they got forceful about making me play with them. I just wasn't interested – it wasn't my thing.

Then I moved to the UK and my brother started dating a beautiful young lady who became an older sister to me. She would often compliment me on features I hadn't paid attention to before. Suddenly, I became interested in makeup and clothes that were less baggy and heels and being more "girly" and she was more than willing to show me the ropes. She would often say I had lovely legs (I hated my skinny, spotty legs) so I started to wear fewer trousers and more skirts. She was light-skinned thinking about it but she loved my skin. She would often look at my face and say how cute I am and she demonstrated this by always taking me everywhere she went. I was known as her "handbag" simply because wherever she went, (even if I was too young to go) I went. Her friends became my big sisters too because we came as a packaged deal.

I was 12 when they met and started dating, so a lot of her comments were foundational to how I saw myself. She continued my dad's practice of constantly reminding me that I was worth so much simply by being me. I didn't have to be funny or tall or anything other than who I am for her to think I was the business. Even when I would beat myself down for not being "this" or "that", she would look at me and say "Tolu – everything about you is just perfect. From your cute eyes to your beautiful smile and even your small skinny self – just perfect". I was this skinny, barely developed girl but she would speak to me and about me like I was so much more. I was simply enough. I still remember her telling someone off who said something derogatory to me in her presence and coming to me afterwards to say they were jealous because my smile always lights up a room.

This was what I knew as a child and that formed the foundation of my understanding when it came to my complexion. Surely this shows then how unprepared I then was to have this hottie (back to current day) sit across from me and confuse me with the words that were coming out of his mouth. True to his words though, he dropped me and I noticed from his Instagram feed that his likes and comments were on ladies clearly more desirable than I – that desired set of "light-skinned girls".

Yet this guy was not a bad guy. He was intelligent, ambitious, focused, and funny – did I mention hot? This made it worse for me, because I couldn't just write him off as yet another silly guy. I had to pause and examine what was happening. Why would someone so intelligent dismiss someone they admit finding attractive and feel connected to (as he said he was) simply because they are brown-skinned? Is that the only reason or is there an underlying issue here? Why have we been conditioned to think that lighter is better? I decided to learn what made him think this way. I genuinely don't believe it was self-hate. Maybe it was simply preference—like how you want something you don't have or find things that are different attractive.

"Our image of perfection is the reason we reject ourselves – the way we are – and why we don't accept others the way they are"
Don Miguel Ruiz

I was reading a book by a well-known actress who started the book saying she was light and as a result, everyone who saw her would complement her on how beautiful she was. Why did her being light skinned automatically translate to her being beautiful? Why is that even a thing we consider in the grand scheme of all things beautiful?

I have chosen to focus on the issue of being lighter-skinned simply because I have since had my eyes open to the fact that this is still a prevalent issue and one that has condemned many a damsel whose only crime is the tone of their skin (I still love my lighter-skinned beauties, of course). After this episode, I realised that a lot of young ladies out there are "toning" in an effort to get lighter skin. But this is missing the fundamental issue – your self-worth and self-esteem shouldn't be based on something as flimsy as your skin tone. I was sad to see the hottie go, but I had to remind myself that I am worth knowing and there are plenty of others who would want a piece of whatever I'm selling.

The fact that I am just dealing with this at this late stage of my life journey convinces me not to let this be a showstopper. In fact, I'm going to focus my confused energy on making myself even more fabulous (booked a facial with the girls – yes!), learning something new (pick up a book) and wowing the long-sighted guys around me (go me!). I am enough as I am – because (not despite) of my hue! For everyone else who has been lied to that lighter is better – lets work on relearning (say this with me) I AM ENOUGH – ME and MY HUE.

5

SAGE ADVICE

Focusing on all the attention you are not getting (or even the wrong attention you keep getting) can make you want to control the outcome of your next encounter. It can become the sole thing that consumes your every interaction. You just want to be off the market already, so you become almost addicted to searching (without seeming like you're searching) for YOUR person. This is particularly dangerous because it takes the focus off you and your amazingness and puts the focus on a stranger whose intent you do not know.

Our mothers were right when they warned us about letting strangers in when we were children. It's not because of a lack of trust in humanity; they just didn't know the intentions of the people that came to the door. To get access, that stranger would have to prove himself/herself. Now, as adults, we discard that sage advice and assume every stranger, every man, has good intentions just because they smell good, talk slick, and smile nice.

Often, we don't realise we have slipped into this destructive pattern. It's natural to desire companionship – that person that gets you and who you can be your true self with, knowing you are completely loved and accepted. We want it in the here and now – someone we can touch, cuddle, kiss, and do nothing or everything with – OUR person. There is no shame in wanting this. It's not desperate, especially when you feel ready to give and receive love and are actively seeking and praying for it. It only becomes dangerous when we focus on finding our worth in someone else, and stop trying to learn who we are and what we are made to do.

I was so excited when one of my girlfriends got engaged and started planning a destination wedding somewhere in Asia. She had found that wonderful thing we're all looking for – HER person. I am one of those people that truly loves love. I always want to rejoice with those who are celebrating, so I was happy to travel 3,000 miles to witness her big day. I made travel plans with another friend of mine, and off we went.

On arrival, we went to check into our room before exploring the hotel. I was really keen to take in the sights but little did I know that the most beautiful sight of all was going to be in that hotel lobby.

As we were checking in, the hotel receptionist stopped

talking and seemed to freeze. She was staring at something behind us. Curious, I turned around and that's when I saw him. My knees wobbled, and my stomach did a quick backflip somersault. Now, I have to describe this beauty. He was a six-foot-two, mocha-coloured, well-built, well-dressed, sweet-smelling sizzler. When I learned he knew my roommate, my excitement level blew the scale into tiny, heart-shaped pieces.

"It is natural to desire companionship…YOUR person. It is not desperate!"
Tolu Adesina

I should pause here and say that before this trip I had been experiencing a major drought in my love life. I had just come out of a dead-end situation (I can't refer to it as a relationship) that should never have started in the first place. I was eager (not desperate!) to find someone who wanted me and who I wanted back. I find that I am unlike many other women in that I don't get constant attention from men. In fact, I rarely get approached and so, when I finally meet someone, and I connect with him, I take it seriously. It's a rare event, so I don't joke around with it. Now with that background set – let's get back to the sizzler.

Over the day, we formed part of a group that toured the city. Though we made eye contact and were introduced, we never spoke to each other. He was clearly the subject of interest to a couple of ladies who managed to attach themselves to our group. They would laugh at his every comment, and one kept finding excuses to reach over and touch him. Unnecessary drama gives me a migraine, so I found myself staying away from him. My friend had given me a bit of a background on him. Even though she wasn't sure if he was single or not, I wanted a migraine-free trip and decided he would make good eye-candy but nothing else.

Lollipop and TM joined us later and that's when the fun really started. They are some of my absolute favourite people and having not seen them for a while, we quickly settled into catching up and doing us. Lollipop noticed the sizzler right away (she's truly my heart-sister and knows me so well) but cautioned me to play it cool. If he liked what he saw, he would approach. In the meantime, we chilled and hung out and enjoyed being around each other. Over that weekend, the sizzler had many opportunities to be around me and he finally seized one to strike up a conversation. We ended up getting on so well that he started neglecting his friends to hang out with me. On the day of the wedding, he stuck to me like white on rice and we ended up dancing the night away — literally! We didn't leave until nearly six in the morning and as we had to be up with the wedding party to go on a day trip at nine, we decided we would just stay awake. Our plan was to go to our respective rooms, change and meet back in the hotel lobby to play games with some friends and continue talking. By that point, everyone could see we were clearly into each other. Our little group agreed to the plan and off I went to my room to change into a more comfortable outfit.

On getting back to the hotel lobby, he was nowhere to be found (I took longer than the ten minutes agreed) and so I called TM to see where he and Lollipop were. They had gotten tired of waiting and decided to try and get a couple of hours of sleep. At that moment, I decided to call my roomie to let her know I was heading back to the room so she could stay up for us to have a girly chat and I could tell her all about the sizzler. As I was heading up, I got a message from the sizzler that the party had moved to one of the rooms as the hotel didn't want them in the lobby being noisy. I thought nothing of it and headed up to the room he gave me instead. When he opened the door, I didn't hear any noise, but I just assumed everyone would be there. I was wrong. Apparently, the party was for two!

Over the years, I have built up a deep appreciation for accountability. For those who shy away from it because they are scared of people in their business I will say this – your accountability circle doesn't need to be big. It just needs to be people that you trust, respect and who accept you. They have to be people with principles you aspire to and who are not afraid to correct you in love. I am deeply appreciative of my accountability circle and each time I have gotten myself in trouble, it has been because I deliberately ignored or neglected to make myself accountable.

Back to my private party. Alarm bells rang but they were muted because the sizzler had been such a gentleman all night. Still, I decided to let my roomie know where I was, since I had told her I was coming back to the room. So, I walked into the suite, picked up the phone and dialed my room. As I did so, I told the sizzler what I was doing but before he could respond, my roomie had picked up and I told her what had happened and where I was. All she wanted to know was if I was coming back anytime soon or if she should go to bed. I figured it was OK for her to go to bed, but instead I just said, "Whichever works." I got off the phone and was shocked by the angry look on the face of my unexpected host.

I was taken aback so I had to ask what was wrong. He sat down on the other side of the room to me and said "Nothing – I just thought I was dealing with an adult." I was so confused. What was he on about? What's the big deal about letting someone who was waiting on me know my plans had changed and why?

Apparently calling my roomie to say I wasn't coming to the room was not an issue, but telling her where I was and who I was with was an issue and a sign that I was not "grown." I didn't even have time to feel insulted before he suddenly switched tacks and offered me a drink (I asked for tea). He acted like nothing happened. I truly thought I had imagined that moment because after making my tea, he walked over, served me and then sat next to me. Before I knew it, we were back talking and laughing. We spoke about so many things and he was respectful, so I felt relaxed. At one point we realised it was already eight in the morning and we would have to go get ready for the general trip, but we were enjoying each other's company so we just kept going.

"Scars remind us where we've been – they don't have to dictate where we are going"
Joe Mantegna

What happened next was like something out of a bad movie. I mentioned that I should probably head back to my room, as I would need time to get ready to make the call-time set for the trip. He suggested waiting a few more minutes and said he would make some more tea. He then got up and put the little hotel kettle on. The next thing I knew, he was kneeling in front of me (I was sitting with my legs tucked under me wearing a long flowing maxi dress). I laughed because it was so unexpected and the next thing I know, he was kissing me. Now – if you've been following, you already know I found him very attractive and having spent the day and night with him, I clearly liked him. But this was so unexpected that I pushed him away. It was literally a case of going from 10 to 1000 in the blink of an eye. I needed more warning – more romance – more something – but you can't just go from talking about work to snogging my face off. I need more warming up. I don't think he expected my reaction because the next thing I know, he's pulling my legs out from under me while trying to get my dress up. I was in utter shock. I couldn't actually speak. All I could do was push him away and shake my head. He then said, "Don't be such a child – haven't you had a nice time?"

Say what now? What does having a nice night in each other's company have to do with what you are doing right now? I found my voice then enough to say NO – please stop. I told him I don't do that (not sure why I used those words) but he laughed and said "Don't worry – you'll enjoy it." I think that's when I felt fear. I went from thinking he was an angel to looking at his face and thinking "Is this really happening?" He was being super aggressive and had actually pinned my hands down so I would stop struggling.

There are few moments that I can say in my life where I felt like I was having an out-of-body experience, but this was definitely one of them. It was like I was watching the scene from far away and talking to the girl telling her to stand up or push him away. He was way stronger than I was, and he was extremely forceful about trying to get under my dress. He said a few things that morning that still make me feel uneasy even now as I remember and type this. But in that moment – during that out-of-body experience – I heard my voice calmly say "You're not a monster are you? – You won't hurt me will you?" For some reason my words and the tone in which I spoke hit him and he looked at me and said "Of course I'm not a monster." Then I said, calmly again, "Please stop. Let me stand up – you're hurting me and this position you're holding me in is painful." He looked confused, lessening his grip on me so I could free one hand and I softly pushed him away. He leaned back. I saw my opportunity then to jump up and I did - nearly falling over in the process. He caught me and said I shouldn't leave. This time, I felt more in control as I was on my feet, even though he had a tight grip on my arm. I said my roomie's name and reminded him that she was waiting for me. I think saying her name is what finally did it. He then said he would let me out and walk me back to the room and because talking to him had been working, I kept speaking calmly and even laughed though my heart was beating so loud I was sure he could hear it.

Thinking back – anyone watching us on the hotel cameras would have thought we were a young couple having a good time as he walked me back. But when I got into the lift (I asked him not to follow me in) the full realisation hit me, and I started shaking uncontrollably. I barely made it to my room before calling Lollipop and she quickly woke TM up. When they got me calm enough to speak and I could tell them what happened, TM (my cool, laid-back friend) was so mad and demanded to know what room he was in so he could be dealt with.

In that moment though, all I felt was shame. Shame that I didn't see it coming. Shame that I put myself in that position. Shame at the thought that most people would question why I was in his room alone in the first place. Shame that I had made such a public display of my affections for him. Shame that my ability to discern good people from "bad" people had failed simply because he was cute in a three-piece suit. But aside from that – I was extremely thankful. This story could have ended much worse (and I'm so conscious that for a lot of women it does). I have never felt as helpless or out of control as I did that night. I trusted him. I didn't see him as the stranger my mummy warned me of. All I saw was the potential of finding MY person that I gave access to a stranger and didn't pace myself. When I next saw him, he acted like nothing had happened. It was so mind boggling that I ended up following him around as he ignored me trying to get a sense that he knew what I knew. Thank God for amazing friends. TM, Lollipop and my roomie never doubted me for a second and they formed a shield around me until the trip was over, ensuring that I had many more positive memories than that one experience.

But I learnt something that trip. I learnt that just someone looks great, doesn't mean I have to take the bait. It turns out that he was married and was just looking for a holiday fling. When I seemed to not take the bait, he wanted to forcefully take it. He had invested his time and was determined to get a return on his investment. The day after this event he had another girl he was pouring his attention on – like nothing happened! The sage advice of letting others prove their intentions before you jump in still rings as true for you at 28 or 38 as it did at 8. For those with pure intentions, it will help build a strong foundation and for those with less than stellar intent, it might just be the wall of protection you need to keep the wolves out.

I am sure for some, reading this chapter might have dug up some emotions that are uncomfortable at best and soul shattering at its worst. As such, I don't want to move on without leaving a word of prayer for those who really need one. The scriptures in Proverbs 18:3 says "When wickedness arrives, shame's not far behind". This experience, though shared in a light manner, really left me shaken and has stayed with me years on. I cannot fathom how others might feel. The words in verse 14 of the same book and chapter sum it up: adversity can really leave your spirit crushed. My words will never suffice, so I will leave you with a prayer. My heart's cry is that the words in Proverbs 18:10 will become life to you. That scripture says that the name of God is a place of protection where we can run to and be safe. As you call the name of Jesus, I pray that you find safety and protection. I pray you find healing for your broken heart and crushed spirit. I love the lyrics of Tasha Cobbs' song "Break Every Chain" because its words are scriptural and true. There is power in the name of Jesus and that power can (and will) break every chain of guilt, shame, loss, un-forgiveness, stolen youth, anger and every wickedness done to and against you. There is power in that name to heal. That name remains a strong tower. Please hold on to that.

I once read somewhere that seeds grow in silence while trees fall with great noise and that has stuck with me ever since. Destruction brings with it great noise and crushing while creation is quiet. I pray that as you read these words and call upon that name and allow Him to start creating in you a new future, you have the strength and fortitude to trust in the power of His gentle embrace. He sets free, speaks, heals, and rebuilds even in those seemingly quiet, unseen moments.

6

HIDDEN

When we long for a life without difficulties, remind us that oaks grow strong in contrary winds and diamonds are made under pressure
Peter Marshall

All my stories so far have been about relationships that didn't work out. You'd be forgiven if you thought this was all leading towards a love story—a story about how I met my one true love, which made all the previous experiences worthwhile. But I'll have to save that for another book. Not all my experiences were bad or ridiculous, but I've definitely learned what rejection looks, feels, and smells like. As such this next encounter is one, which really blew (and still blows)

my mind and led to me penning this book.

I was minding my business one afternoon when I was dragged (literally) into the path of a young gentleman I will label Mr. Cool. The night before this collision, I had gone out for drinks with a newly married friend of mine and we were talking about love, marriage, and business. During our conversation, I asked her how she knew this guy was the one and how, if at all, marriage had changed her view. She said she knew he was someone who was note-worthy because he paid attention to her interests (which are very wide reaching) and had immediately embarked on empowering her to do more in her business. I wasn't expecting that answer - most people would say he was sweet, romantic, and so on - but she was very specific with her response. She is someone I would call a dreamer, in the best possible way. She has grand ideas and has always got her hands in several pots. She has started many successful businesses and has a passion for helping people who don't have a voice to be heard.

When she responded with her comment, it hit me that she recognised her mate because she knew who she was and what it is she loves to do. You can't be around her without feeling inspired and excited. Even when she's having a hard time, she is still strategising and planning the next venture.

We talked about a lot of things that night, but what she said about her husband stayed with me. On our way home, she asked if I was ready for a relationship. Funny enough, I had walked away from a dead-end situation months back and had taken time to heal, forgive (him and myself), and move on. I had no residual feelings for him. Instead, I was focused on building myself. But when she asked, I hesitated. I wanted to give as honest an answer as possible. Finally, I said I was ready but I didn't want another false start. I am ready to meet the right person - not just yet another guy. I was feeling pretty good about where I was mentally and emotionally for the first time in a long time and I didn't want anything or anyone who would derail that. I then joked and asked if she had someone that fit the bill in mind. She casually laughed and said she'll think about it. Then we parted for the night, having laughed more than we ate or drank.

The next morning, a different friend called to ask me out. I was feeling a little groggy but agreed. And that's how I met Mr. Cool. This meeting was definitely unexpected and I had no prior warning that this was coming. Here I was, standing in front of a guy who I thought was really cute. Then he started talking and I immediately fell in love.

"People generally see what they look for
and hear what they listen for"
Harper Lee

For every physical attribute that I could describe (and he is aesthetically pleasing), what knocked me off my feet was his mind. We seemed to think the same, yet so different. I was so impressed by him I felt like I was going to burst. This guy was just not like any other I had met before. He was cute like the others yes, but in the short time we hung out, I was challenged in my spirit to do more than I was doing with my dreams, talents, and abilities. I had always wanted to write, to create and tell stories, but I always found a way to talk myself out of doing so. I also know I have the gift of encouragement, and have always wanted to do something in education to help young people. Once again, though, I always talked myself out of trying. Speaking to him, I knew I had found someone I could truly let loose around. There is only one other person I have ever felt connected to in that way and he is still one of my closest friends. But this guy was simply yummy and he was fully into me from the jump so I allowed myself to get carried away.

Unfortunately, for some reason, he suddenly went cold. Normally, I would just shake it off. But this I just couldn't understand. It wasn't just about physical attraction. Few men can stimulate my mind as well as my eyes. But alas - he was emotionally unavailable and didn't want a relationship. Other things mattered more to him right then, and that was where he wanted to concentrate. As he walked out of my life, all I could focus on was the feeling that I had nothing to offer. Having someone that seemed of a like mind who couldn't appreciate me was devastating.

I felt bone weary. I hadn't wanted another false start or dashed hopes. I didn't feel like looking at the big picture or on the bright side this time. I didn't think anything would change with the next guy or the one after that. I was feeling angry at everything I was (I internalise when things don't go as planned). And then one morning, I had an encounter and I haven't been the same ever since.

"Life tried to crush her, but only succeeded in creating a diamond"

John Mark Green

On this fateful day, at my usual time of six in the morning, I logged in to my church's morning prayer webinar. I didn't actually feel like praying. I dialed in anyway, but turned the volume to low and started lamenting and warring within myself again. I lay there thinking of all the things I felt I was not and how I'm always passed over and I have to fight ten times as hard as the next person to get less than half of what they seemed to get so easily. I am a natural giver and I have watched people take and then go and give or invest their love, affection, and time in others, completely shattering me in the process. Often without a second look at the damage they left behind. I don't give to receive (I know better) but I do have my moments when I feel low (despite being able to put a good face on) about how I am treated, especially by those I love, knowing if they had a choice they would likely choose others over me.

This was my dramatic thought process that morning. I couldn't stop the lamentations that kept flowing. Negative thoughts are like a magnet: as soon as I thought of one, another three examples would flash up and force out every positive thought. But then, suddenly, I saw a picture of myself hidden in a vault looking out at everyone else being showcased and admired and fawned over. I heard clearly "You are my treasure hidden in my vault. You are not like everyone else."

What??? What am I supposed to do with this?? I was so confused. I knew I was having some sort of a spiritual encounter in the middle of my pity party, but I didn't know what to do with it. I immediately started asking questions and challenging the vision. I don't want to be in a vault! Why should I be hidden when others are loved and celebrated? Why me? Put someone else in the vault – surely, it's my time to shine now. I have been through enough in my life and suffered enough surely. However, what God revealed to me in that moment and since then, has remade me and is still rebuilding me. I am not the same woman I was before this episode and my thought patterns are not the same either. My entire perspective changed, and now I have a different worldview.

In that moment, I saw a picture of a jewellery shop. Hundreds and thousands of people were walking past. Most would stop and admire the jewels in the window and these jewels would sparkle in return. To the item in the vault, that looked like the ultimate - the prized final destination. Who doesn't want to be admired? But God spoke to me then and said "No one puts their true treasure in the shop window where anyone can reach, touch, handle and discard without care". Then I looked again and saw the shop assistants in the middle of the shop by the glass cabinet protecting their higher value jewels. Very few people make it to this section unless they are looking for something different from what everyone else has. To view these jewels, you have to ask the shop assistant to unlock the cabinet for you to see. Only then, can you then touch them or try them on. For most people, this is where they stop. But a few know to ask to see what's inside the vault. Those few are the sheikhs, kings and princes, the truly wealthy who want something rare that no one else has or has touched and mishandled. Something of true value and worth. Something pure. Then I saw myself (sitting pretty) in the vault.

I nearly passed out. You don't understand. I can think of a million other women more deserving of that honour than I. I am not pure! I have been unfaithful to God so many times and in so many ways. I am a work in progress. Yet I heard Him clearly that morning that I am His rare treasure and He would not let me go to just anyone – only a king. I was blown away. I couldn't even see myself the way God just told me I am. I had betrayed Him by having sex with a past boyfriend – surely, He remembers that. I had been disobedient so many times to His calling and assignment. I had put others before Him. I had wallowed in self-pity. I had been rude and mean and obnoxious. I had done terrible things even after knowing Christ as the one true God. Surely, He doesn't mean me. Yes, I have repented, but I was still so burdened by the fact that I was not perfect and had disappointed God over and over again. That's when God decided, in his awesome mercy and grace, to walk me on this journey to seeing myself the way He sees me.

I wish I had had this encounter years ago – I would not have made the mistakes I made or opened doors to people I shouldn't have, but I am learning that all my missteps give me a message and an insight that is truly unique in helping others avoid the pits I fell into in ignorance.

I am flawed like most, yet treasured by this amazing God. I am hidden in the vault but still showcased to bring light, healing, and a representation of God's manifest grace to women (and men) who like me feel condemned at every turn - often by their own actions and choices. I have shared and exposed my stories to show you that I am not perfect. Yet here I am — a vault item. There is such power in that. I am not like those who have had it easy. I had to fight to get everything I have, but it has built tenacity in me. I fall constantly but you must never count me out of the race because I – must – win. I will win MY race – not yours. I'm constantly being reminded that the race is not to the swift or the battle to the strong – but time and chance (divine, supernatural) happens to us all.   That scripture in Ecclesiastes 9:11 fills me with such hope because it levels the playing field. My race will end in my showcasing, not for me to shine, but for me to be a blazing pointer to God's incredible mercy, grace and love.

7

___

VAULT ITEM

A diamond is a chunk of coal that did really well under pressure
Henry Kissinger

The first thing to note is that not every jewellery shop has a vault. Most actually only cater to front-of-house (FOH) and middle-tier (MT) jewels. That's the limit of their capacity. Front-of-house jewels are the shop window jewels that anyone can see as they walk past. Middle tier jewels are the ones displayed in a locked cabinet in the middle of the shop. You have to ask the shop assistant before you can try on the MT jewel, as they have more value than the FOH items. That's normally all most jewellery shops offer. If you're a vault item looking for validation from every jewellery shop, you'll be so disappointed.

FOH items tend to be what I call sparklers. They sparkle for a time before fizzling out. There is no real substance to them. Anyone walking past can see, touch, and try on a FOH sparkler. Whether they have money or not, and whether they have the intention of buying or not, the sparkler is theirs to play with and discard once they're done. There's nothing unique about the FOH sparkler. Every jewellery shop has them in their dozen. They are not rare or uncommon and tend to be of less value than a MT stone. Put under pressure, a FOH jewel will lose its sparkle and dullen with time.

Given the rarity and cost of jewels, it is only to be expected that there would be more FOH/MT jewels than there are vault items. You are not so rare if you are common now are you? To put a vault item on the shop floor, you would need to put it behind a glass display made of the same tough materials as a vault would be. And even then you would have to protect it with state-of-the-art security – the type you would only see in a James Bond movie.

"The best things in life are life. The second best are very expensive"
Coco Chanel

You can understand then, that for a jewellery shop to have a vault filled with rare gems, they would need to be a shop of repute and with a lot of resources. Just imagine the cost of security. When Samer Halimeh NY (a boutique jewellery store) opened up their flagship boutique in London, the press reported build costs of £10 million. Their security includes bulletproof windows, CCTV cameras, motion sensors, and a 12 tonne, bombproof vault. They are reported to showcase some of their collection behind a 30mm bullet proof glass with their rarest pieces only available to view in private (read: vault). One of the many items deep within their vault is a 20-carat diamond worth £20million as at that time. It is understandable then that not every jewellery shop can afford to hold vault items. As a vault item, that should be the start of you feeling yourself.

Next, not everyone makes it towards the vault. The jewellery boutique described above is clearly not for the average shopper. The average shopper cannot afford a £20 million diamond. They do not have the ability to buy or even care for it in the long term. Vault items are not only practical and extremely valuable, but also great for investments, which is why they are tucked away.

I don't know how many people grew up in homes where your mum had one or two pieces of gold, or pieces of fine china. These items of value were not brought out for everyday guests or events. Your mum would not put on her gold jewellery to go to the supermarket or to take you to school. In fact, as kids, you were never, under any circumstance, allowed to go near where she stored these items. You only saw them on occasions when she brought them out to clean them, or for those special events where she would wear them, knowing she would be noticed and admired. Your finest china came out only when you had those VIP guests. That is because of the value we place on these items: while they are practical, they are also high in value and shouldn't be treated with contempt.

Let's look at some of the things that constitute vault items:

- Gold bullions

- Precious metals (e.g. platinum, palladium, rhodium, plutonium)

- Nature's most unique gems

- Rare gemstones (e.g. emerald, ruby, sapphire, opal)

- Valuable assets (e.g. important documents such as shares/bond certificates)

- Diamonds

This is, by no means, an exhaustive list, but it should start giving you a flavour of how special and diverse vault items are. Precious metals like platinum are as practical as they are valuable. For example, you can't buy plutonium. If you could buy it, in 2008 you could pay up to $10,000 for an ounce. Today, it is literally priceless. In that same period, platinum was trading at about $1,600 an ounce; gold at $900 an ounce; while rhodium is so rare I couldn't find anywhere that could put a price on it. They are valued so highly because they are:

- Rare

- Pure

- Have practical use

- Have commercial/economic use

Metals like silver, for example, are used for currency (e.g. pound sterling) while platinum is used for everything from flat screen TVs to diesel fuel. Vault items also have great economic use, as they can be used to hedge against inflation or economic downturns. These are not items to be dismissed lightly. The moment you make a vault item common, it loses its high market value (Aluminium is an example of this).

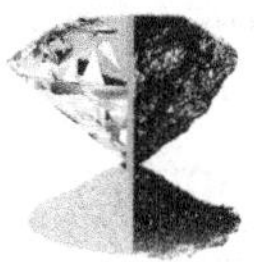

"Don't lose a diamond while chasing glitter"
Author Unknown

Knowing this, do you think vault items need to be envious of FOH or MT? Should they reduce themselves to the same level as these other items? Surely not. Vault items simply need to stay in their lane being fabulous. They are not for everyone - they can't be. If they look at the FOH or MT items to validate their worth, it might seem there's something wrong with them. A vault item might only get one or two customers a month, whereas thousands look at an FOH jewel.

I have spent my life (until recently) not realising I am a vault item. This has caused me to look with serious envy at the FOH and MT gems, wishing I were like them. Many times I have even cheapened myself just to try and get the same attention and validation. I compromised, gave sacred things away for free (even when I knew better), and even felt rejected when I was passed over by the average man who didn't realise my worth. I didn't realise I was special and hidden. I didn't see myself as so valuable that I couldn't just be used in any kind of way. I am meant to be showcased and to have the world take notice. This could be in raising godly children, or in setting people's minds free from the bondage of self-doubt or the paralysis of fear. Whatever the platform God has in mind, I have been hidden in the vault so that I can be prepped and readied for the challenge. To be hidden in the vault is extremely special.

That sounds so arrogant now, but God's love and plan is not restricted to only me. It's an open promise for anyone who calls on His name and draws close to Him. What makes me a vault item isn't anything I have done but simply whose I am. I take no credit for being a vault item because left to my own devices, I would be out in the street leading the pack of FOH jewels.

Writing this book has been a torturous experience because I know how broken I was and I didn't want to expose myself to the world. I wanted to stay hidden, but God promised to shield me, as I became a polished arrow and a sharpened sword in his hand. So I got writing. In fact, the work God has to do on my heart and mind to convince me I am a vault item cannot be covered in the pages of this book. He revealed to me my true nature using the scriptures and like

Isaiah, I replied, "I've worked for nothing. I've nothing to show for a life of hard work. Nevertheless, I'll let God have the last word. I'll let him pronounce his verdict" (Isaiah 49:4). Because no matter what I did yesterday, or last year, He is whispering in my ear and heart that He has forgiven me. He is opening my eyes so I can see myself the way He sees me. He tells me that He put me to work from the day I was born. The moment I entered the world He named me. He gave me speech that would cut and penetrate. He kept his hand on me to protect me. He made me His straight arrow and hid me in His quiver. He said to me, "You're my dear servant, Tolu, through whom I'll shine" (Isaiah 49:1-3). He looks at me, not through the lens of my mistakes and hardened heart, but through the lens of his love, sacrifice, and purpose. I bear his name now truly - not just in my words but also now with my whole being. I have found my identity in Him and know that he is my Father. What an honour for me in God's eyes! That God should be my strength! And make me a light to the nations (Isaiah 49:5-6). Your perspective can truly alter your reality and now I am convinced God will protect me and hide me as I cut and penetrate for His glory to shine.

And I know for a fact he wants to do the same for you, too - if only you'll let Him.

8

PRUNED TO PERFECTION

Better a diamond with a flaw than a pebble without
Confucius

I have come to learn that a key trait of vault items such as rare gemstones is that they take a long time to form. The transformation from FOH to vault item will not happen overnight. You will need to be open to God refining you (changing your heart, thoughts, words, and everything in between) and allow the Holy Spirit to birth something new in you. What I am saying is, if you are willing to start this journey with God and allow him to use your circumstances to reveal who you really are and can be, you will, like Paul, be taken on an adventure where you will be showcased as God's personal representative (Acts 9:15).

Let's look at the sapphire as an example to illustrate how we can be transformed into a vault item. A sapphire can take millions of years to form and are often formed during the transformation of igneous rocks. They are, more often than not, affected by the elements around them and develop imperfections. These imperfections are like our fingerprint - they are what make the gemstones unique. Finding one without imperfections is extremely rare, and it would probably be rather small. Their colour is actually derived from the various elements around them as they are formed so their true beauty and value lies in their imperfections. This is something that blows my mind.

I can understand that a vault item needs to be pure, but mixing purity with imperfection is something my mind couldn't fathom for the longest time. You see, I had always thought that to be pure meant to have never fallen or made mistakes. I remember an occasion during a worship event. A young man approached me with a message saying he had seen a vision of me on a stage giving a talk on purity. I laughed. I mean - I actually laughed in his face. Me? Talking about purity? How is that going to work? I am as impure as they come. Surely he meant someone else? I have slipped and fallen and slid so many times while trying to attain purity. To start with, in my mind, to be pure you had to be a virgin and untouched in any way. That was definitely not me. Also, your mind had to be holy - always heaven focused. Well, there have been many a time when I saw a fine looking brother and definitely had impure thoughts. I am by no means a candidate to be signing up to give talks on purity.

Somewhere along the line (after I got this message on a purity platform), God started me on this journey where he started working on my mind and changing the way I saw myself. He directed me to the book of Esther and there, He captured my heart and reduced me to tears. Esther 2:15 says:

"Esther, just as she was, won the admiration of everyone who saw her."

As I read that verse, all I saw was "just as she was". I can't explain it, but I couldn't move past that line. As I said above, I am a vault item only on the basis of whose I am. But still, for God to say He's taking me - just as I am - floored me.

The decision to explore Christianity came after a long battle with my anger at God and a pull to learn more. During my walk with Christ, I have fallen multiple times and after making one mistake, then two, I soon found myself unable to reconcile the person I thought I was becoming (Christian, grounded in my faith) with the things I found myself doing (misbehaving and generally acting the fool). When the smoke finally cleared, and I was able to walk away and prayerfully start over, I was consumed with a desire to help others see that our daily walk with Christ is only by grace - not because we are stronger than the next person or have our act together and all figured out. I had misrepresented Christ in a way I never thought possible and I was thoroughly ashamed. Yes, I knew I was forgiven, but forgiving myself doesn't come easy to me, so I channeled my energy into helping others - particularly young women - avoid and (if need be) face without condemnation the realities of bad choices. As I figured out a way to do this on a wider scale, God has been working on me with regards to my speech, the way I carry myself, how I react to situations (one of the many ways I misrepresented Him) and many other areas of my life.

Being in the vault presents the benefit and opportunity to be pruned. I don't know about you, but I hate being corrected in public. I would rather be called to a private place to receive my correction. The aspect of my character that needs work isn't the part of me I want highlighted and magnified for all to see. Being a vault item does not mean you will have no imperfections, but to become exquisite, heat treatment is needed to bring out our true clarity, cut, and colour. Instead of dulling your radiance with malicious gossip, fill your mouth with praise and watch the transformation that follows. Instead of being quick to anger and judgement, be filled instead with an even temperament born out of being filled with the Holy Spirit and looking at issues through His lens. Learn to have a good attitude in the face of being mistreated. It's all part of the pruning process.

Imperfections are magnified under a spotlight so the season before your discovery and showcasing is so important. It is not a time to complain, but instead a time to develop and be developed. Spending the time moaning and grumbling stunts your growth. Even if you don't understand the manner of your pruning or the timing and length of it, don't begrudge the process and what it is looking to birth in you. Often, I have thought I was ready, that the time of being pruned or hidden was over. But when I had a go of it on my own, the result was heartache and pain with very little to show for the suffering endured.

God truly does accept us as we are, but He never leaves us the same. You will find love as you are, but in love God will prune you to imperfect perfection. Delays, disappointments, and difficulties all help shape us into who we need to be. One of my favourite scriptures is in Romans 5:3-5:

"There's more to come: We continue to shout our praise even when we're hemmed in with troubles, because we know how troubles can develop passionate patience in us, and how that patience in turn forges the tempered steel of virtue, keeping us alert for whatever God will do next. In alert expectancy such as this, we're never left feeling short-changed. Quite the contrary—we can't round up enough containers to hold everything God generously pours into our lives through the Holy Spirit!"

The NLT version puts it this way:

"We can rejoice, too, when we run into problems and trials, for we know that they help us develop endurance. And endurance develops strength of character, and character strengthens our confident hope of salvation. And this hope will not lead to disappointment. For we know how dearly God loves us, because he has given us the Holy Spirit to fill our hearts with his love."

This scripture makes me feel good because I too have had many problems and troubles. It shows me what I should be doing. Instead of screaming and crying, I need to build roots and character and never lose hope. I am a passionate person, and I used to think I needed to be gentler in order to be a virtuous woman. But now I know I can be passionately patient – not mute or suppressing my feelings and thoughts – but tempered, strong, and alert. I have been promised that my hope will not be disappointed. I will not be left feeling cheated and short-changed because God knows that unrelenting disappointment makes you heartsick but good breaks turn your life around. (Proverbs 13:12)

Even better is knowing that nothing, no delay or disappointment, is wasted in God. Every one of the issues I have experienced has taught me compassion and while I am being healed, God is helping me bring healing to others. I often feel like I have experienced certain things just so I can connect better with others and grow with them. Having experienced these things, I can say "I might not know exactly how you feel but I connect with you and you are not alone."

I have often cried to God to spare me from certain scenarios, but it's exactly those scenarios that cause me to grow the most. God has used some of my darkest moments to help others who are struggling. He has provided me with the words needed to support those who are going through pain and emotional trauma. We can be sure that every detail in our lives of love for God is worked into something good (Romans 8:28). 2 Corinthians 1:3-4 puts it best:

"All praise to the God and Father of our Master, Jesus the Messiah! Father of all mercy! God of all healing counsel! He comes alongside us when we go through hard times, and before you know it, he brings us alongside someone else who is going through hard times so that we can be there for that person just as God was there for us."

I know I am still being formed (and the work will not stop) but God was showing me that, just as I am, he was going to showcase me to bring healing to others. To be there for others as He has been there and is still there for me. He will keep refining me so that I can be someone worthy of admiration. All my scars and imperfections will only add to my high value and set me apart from others. But just as I have my unique fingerprint, so do you. The same work He has started in me is the same work He wants to do in you. He wants you to know He wants you - just as you are. Come to Him with a repentant heart and let Him remake you.

In Esther 2:17, the scripture says that the king fell in love with Esther far more than with any of his other women or any of the other virgins and was totally smitten by her. Doesn't that gladden your heart to read? A relationship with God and living in obedience earns you the king's love, above all others. Staying close to God means learning the secrets to desirability - if it's guarding your tongue or being more patient or smiling more! Whatever it is, with the help of the Holy Spirit, God wants to give you a platform to pour yourself out in his service and in so doing, shape and mould you into a gem that will win the admiration of all who see you. Your passion, diligence, tenacity, strength, compassion, and feisty spirit make you a weapon in His hands, which He will use to transform you into a rock on which He can build. Your story makes you useful. Your story makes you needed. Your story makes you able.

We must know that waiting does not diminish us; it enlarges us. Romans 8:25 says the longer we wait, the more joyful our expectancy. So you might feel like you are ready to be showcased. Ready for that husband (read: king), ready for that baby, ready for that amazing job, ready for your first million — whatever it is, trust God's timing. This is the hardest thing to do, but what I am learning is that the only purpose I am here to fulfill is His. That means then that he also dictates the timeline. He is the only one able to make the determination of when and where and how. I get frustrated in my wait and often miss his whisperings because I'm caught up in my despair and hopelessness. But He has been telling me to simply trust and surrender.

This is where you can be real and raw with God. He promises to be with us so when things are tough and you're struggling to stay hopeful, tell him. When the going is tough, and you want out of the race, pour yourself out to Him. Jesus, our ultimate model, was not immune to this and cried out for the cup of suffering to pass over him. What comes next though is that he, recognising whose purpose he was really fulfilling, follows with, "Not what I want but what you want" (Luke 22:42). He demonstrates that even in our darkest, rawest moment, when all light has faded and all hope seems lost, not our will but His will be done.

We might never know why our lives have taken the path it has, but my prayer remains that our eyes will be opened to the results God wants to work in and through us. We are a part of His plan and that in itself is incredibly special. You are a beautiful mess and an epic adventure worth embarking on. Bet on yourself. The rarity of your truth is what makes you a symbol of light and hope to those still searching for a way out. Trust this and learn your value as a gem in His vault - it'll help you walk, talk, and think differently. Bishop T.D. Jakes once said it like this: "God will never use what you have lost - he will use what you have left". Don't count yourself out just yet. Often, when we think we have lost, we are really winning.

9

CUT IT OUT

Potential is a priceless treasure, like gold. All of us have gold hidden within,
but we have to dig it out
Joyce Meyer

If you're anything like me, then it is easy for you to receive the forgiveness of others but very hard for you to forgive yourself. I often feel I have to work very hard to earn the forgiveness of others, but it's much harder work to let go when I mess up and forgive myself. To become a vault item and truly start recognising the value God intends for you to have will mean letting go of some things. But it also means forgiving yourself of poor choices made.

We were all created to be vault items. Over and over again, the scriptures highlight to us that God does not make mistakes. That he created us in his own image is the starting point to recognising that we are not, nor were we ever, meant to be mediocre and cheap. One of my favourite descriptions in the Bible of God's mind for us is in Jeremiah 1:5: "Before I shaped you in the womb, I knew all about you. Before you saw the light of day, I had holy plans for you: A prophet to the nations—that's what I had in mind for you." Before we were born, God had a purpose for us (Psalm 57:2 NLT) - this blows my mind. I was born a vault item as I am unique, practical (I have a purpose, don't you know), of high value, and pure through the sacrifice of Jesus Christ. Sin is what caused the separation between what our original purpose is and where we might find ourselves today. Sin is the disconnector that has removed you from the vault and caused you to be mishandled like a common entity.

God, however, wants to place you back in your rightful place and move you back in the vault. To do that, you have to be willing to walk away and completely disconnect from the sin that has held you captive. When God was whispering in my heart to accept being in the vault, I was so aware of my sin and shame. I was full of shame because I had made so many mistakes. I knew God, but I didn't represent him well. I have friends who are so pure - they pray longer and fast more frequently than I. They are chaste and though they have made mistakes, when compared to me - well there is no comparison. What kind of representation of a vault item am I? What value do I add to God's collection of beautiful gems?

I have already mentioned that there are different types of vault items. While different, their common trait is that they are valuable and practical and pure. These traits, I am starting to realise, are not a function of anything the vault items do. It's the value that is placed on them. They have been subjected to intense pressure and scrutiny and severe weathering to achieve their status as valuable. God has placed value on you and me. My value is not dependent on me having never made a mistake (or 15) but on the God who calls me daughter. The intense pressure and heat I have endured have created deposits of immense value to the one who values me: the God who created me and fulfils His purpose in me, who formed me and says He has called me by name and I am His (Isaiah 43:1 NLT) Because I bear his name, I have value. I don't have to earn it by doing anything other than repenting my sins (the disconnector).

True repentance (not going back) and acceptance of God's mercy allows you to accept His open invitation to move you to the vault, even after all your mistakes. To move to your rightful place, you will have to forgive yourself, even though this is one of the toughest things you can do. You are depriving so many others who could learn from you, partner with you, and soar with you, simply because you are ashamed. Daniel puts it this way in chapter 4 verse 27:

"Take my advice: make a clean break with your sins and start living for others. Quit your wicked life and look after the needs of the down-and-out. Then you will continue to have a good life"

I will paraphrase and say cut out whatever is holding you back and start to live in a way that is dependent on God. As rare, valuable, and beautiful as the black opal is, it pales in comparison to the beautiful treasure hidden in you.

I should state that the amazing thing about God is his

willingness to go on a journey with us. The first step of the journey is recognising who He is. Then we can truly see who we are in Him. The blockage for you in seeing yourself as you truly are in Him could be your own insecurities, feelings of pain caused by a traumatic past, feelings of inadequacies or just not feeling worthy of such a grand love. I have been in such a dark place emotionally over the years because of the feeling of not being good enough or being able to hold on to love. I would often feel bypassed by those I wish would choose me. When pitted against others, my expectation is never that I will be chosen. I can rationalise it so well now that even if you were planning to choose me, you will reconsider based on the arguments I would present on why others are better. I am very self-aware (mostly of my faults) and I have also developed over the years the ability to quickly discern when people consider me as just another option. This has led to me feeling most times that I will not receive love that can truly last - not unless I did something to earn and keep that love. A love where I would be chosen over and over based on who I am not just what I can offer.

It is only in recent times that I have been hearing God say clearly to me - especially in the times when I am not chosen by that guy, by that friend, by that mentor, by whomever - "I have chosen you. Do you choose me too? Am I enough?" I am in tears as I write this, because I struggle to accept from anyone that they can and will genuinely choose me - just for me. Not comparing me to others; not looking at what I can offer in return; not looking to discard me if something better comes along - just choosing me as I am. Let me share an example with you.

"It's not what you say out of your mouth that determines your life; it's what you whisper to yourself that has the most power"
Robert Kiyosaki

I remember the day my best friend and her husband called to tell me that they had chosen me to be the godmother to their first child. I will never be able to fully articulate the emotions I felt that day. I had done nothing to deserve such an honour. But yet, here they both were, telling me that they had prayed about it and they both chose me. I rushed off the phone that day and broke down in tears. I couldn't believe they would trust me with their baby girl and choose me to be part of their amazing journey and family.

She had many options - truly wonderful women that also love her - but she chose me, the one who is broken. I felt like she had seen through the weird me to the heart of who I am. Many times over the years, she had demonstrated her love for me. But nothing moved me like that one act. I had never said this to her, but I took her and her amazing hubby's words that day and wrote them on my heart. It remains a great honour to me and one I do not take lightly.

You can see how much of an impact that one phone call had on my psyche. I'm sure neither of them realise how seriously I take my responsibilities as godmother.

Yet God has chosen you. Even if no one else has ever chosen you. Even if everyone you have ever loved has walked away from you. I want you to know that God sees you and He chooses you. Even with your worst act - the moment you asked for His forgiveness, He chose you again. You are His first choice. He trusts you with His purpose and plan. So many people need to hear those words. Let these words resonate deep into your heart because it is the truth. God is not a man that He should lie.

Looking back at your life, you might struggle to see this but the promises of God do not change based on what cards life dealt you or the poor choices you have made. He knows us far better than we know ourselves and He asks us to be sure that every detail in our lives of love for God is worked into something good (Romans 8:28). His word says we should seek God while he's here to be found. Pray to him and abandon your old way of life and thinking. Come back to God who is merciful and lavish with forgiveness (Isaiah 55:6-7). If you do that, He promises us sure, solid and enduring love. He knew all that would happen to you and He still had plans for you. You were on His mind. Nothing you have done; nothing that has been done to you can ever change that. The moment you leave it at His feet - know that He chooses you and wants to make a lasting covenant with you. To establish you and gloriously complete what He started in you. The only thing you have to decide is whether you are going to choose Him, too.

Like God asked me that day - "Am I enough?" My answer remains a yes. So put away all garments of sin and run into His open arms. It doesn't mean I don't still struggle but when I think of who has chosen me, I feel like I got the better end of the deal. Looking at yourself through His eyes is to see yourself as someone with a purpose that can never be changed - not even on your worst day. The key is in who

He is - He is love. He is merciful. He is just. He is kind. He perseveres. He has sacrificed so we can know him. He created us to love us. He is the father to the fatherless. He is the defender of widows. He heals the broken hearted. He opens door of favour and honour no one can shut. He has a purpose for you. He will fulfill that purpose. Just connect.

"You are gold, baby. Solid gold"
Author Unknown

I truly hope you can see what a treasure you are. But now we have to deal with the expectation that everyone else will see your value as well. We're not looking to appeal to everyone, but those few people who make it to the vault get out hearts racing.

Knowing the calibre of people that are allowed into the vault often sets the level of expectation when they approach. They ask to see you and you shine with all the glory you can muster as they examine, compliment and even try on (with gloves of course). When they then settle for an MT stone, the sense of rejection can be crushing. You only get the one a month - how can he come dressed in the best garb, speaking the Queen's English and not recognise the value you carry? Did they spot a flaw? Are you truly a vault item? It can seem in that moment that you were sold a lie. This vault thing doesn't work and you're really not worth that much. You might even decide you're happy switching roles and becoming a MT instead. They still hold value after all. Who needs to be in the vault?

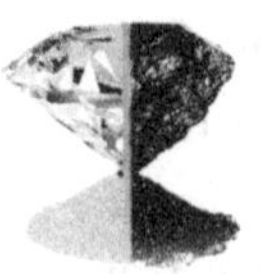

"Do you trust me when my answer is wait?"
God

After Mr. Cool, I went through a whole range of questions. I went to God feeling cheated and deceived. I could see no flaw in the man, so why couldn't I have been chosen? Why was I put back? I love how God loves me though. Honestly. I am such a unique child of His. I throw the most irrational tantrums, yet he never shouts or goes quiet on me. He would always gently reach out to me even when I ignore him. I am truly God's baby - I am starting to accept that now. He speaks to me in ways only my crazy mind can understand - sometimes most potently through Instagram or a random line in scripture that makes sense to no one else but me.

In that moment, while I was busy throwing my toys out of the pram, He asked me if I knew on the morning I met Mr Cool that I would be meeting someone I would end up connecting with. I reluctantly said no. Then He asked me to think back to the start of the year. It had been a very tough year, with challenges ranging from my mum's health, to issues at work, to the breakdown of relationships within my family. He asked me if I knew any of those things were coming before they happened? I said no. He asked if I knew the results of those things before they happened (by the end of the year, my mum was much stronger and healing, God gave me favour at work unexpectedly which was helping me cope with the myriad of issues I was experiencing and the broken relationships are being dealt with thanks to open dialogue) and I had to say no. He then asked me if I knew I would get all the good things and people in my life before I got them and in the way that I got them. I said no. He then whispered to me:

"I am the only one that sees around corners. You just have to trust me and surrender."

Trust and surrender. Two of the toughest things for me to do. I am a control freak. I do not trust others with the end result. I know how much effort I put into things and I have been disappointed enough times to not trust anyone with my happiness and surrendering implies I would have to invest fully in someone else's control/driving of my life. But I kept hearing "Trust and surrender." This is the same God who says he will withhold no good thing from me. Who has promised and has consistently proven to be a father to the fatherless (Psalm 68:5 NLT). Who gave me the Holy Spirit so I can be well and whole (John 14:26). Who has promised that anything I ask for in His name He will do (John 14:14 NIV). Who says he will open doors for me no one can shut (Revelation 3:8 NIV). Who promises to fulfill his promise in me (Psalm 57:2 NLT). If there is anyone worth giving a chance, it's God.

I can't say I have mastered it yet, but I am happy now on this journey with a God who can never fail. I strongly encourage you to do the same. I shared this story to show that just because you understand where you should be in the vault, doesn't mean things become rosy the very next day.

You have to be willing to go on this adventure with God. Trust and surrender. God sees around the corners of your life and He has promised you the best outcome. He will never fail you.

10

COUNT THE COST

Her wounds transformed her into a warrior
R.H. Sin

One key shift God needed to work on with me was my thought patterns. I have already shown how I beat myself up and internalise other people's actions. To claim all that God has for me (and you) then, our minds are one battlefield He has to conquer.

Looking at the customer who approached the vault, viewed, and went on to buy a MT stone, the first instinct is to think he discovered a flaw in you. As with the guy I went to war with God over, I focused on me (my past, my baggage, my flaws) as the reason he chose to walk away. However, I have since come to see that, while he was different from all the guys before him who were truly unserious candidates, he was actually more measured and honest about what he can or cannot afford. Let me explain.

I have already told you that only a king can handle a vault item and kings would only accept the best. The gemstone that no one else has. That rare gem that is hidden in the deepest of vaults and only a select few can afford. As such, the king would need to be someone in a position to buy the gem at its current value and who can afford to pay for the needed upkeep of that gem. That is the insurance money and the yearly appreciation value. Think about it. When a choice is made to buy a vault item, the true cost is more than the initial amount paid. You can't treat a vault item like any other item. Otherwise it will lose its value and shine. You must care for it, insure it, constantly work on it to ensure its purity and value is maintained. That leads me to conclude that anyone buying a vault item must truly weigh the cost before entering into that transaction. Only a fool would rush into it hastily.

When the guy walked away after examining the gem and recognising its true value, the gem can choose to sit there feeling rejected or even decide to cheapen itself and become a MT stone. But an alternative God is presenting is for the gem to be assured of its value and its valuer (God). God wants the buyer to appreciate all of the gem and truly nurture it so it shines brighter and brighter. The potential buyer also could have walked away to sell all he had, like the man in Matthew 13:44-45, so he could come back and buy it. Or he could have gone to put things in place (fix his credit/debt, get a house, settle his business account etc.) to be able to handle and not damage the gem once bought. Don't cheapen yourself with compromise because when he comes back expecting a rare and pure gem, you could be classed as a FOH jewel, and no longer worth the price he was going to pay.

You also don't want some random to have faked his way to the vault, buy you on credit and then treat you like a FOH sparkler. What a waste! Instead of worrying about why someone walked away, spend your time thinking about what differentiates a vault item from a FOH or MT jewel. The Bible says that a wise woman builds her home. What makes a wise woman? What do you want your home to look like? Do you want a home in which you are adored and constantly celebrated? A place where you are accepted and encouraged to be all you can be and win at it all? What do you want to be known for in this chapter of your journey? How will you achieve all this?

"Patience is not the ability to wait, but the ability to keep a good attitude while waiting"
Joyce Meyer

I am so very fortunate to have the best pastors and spiritual parents anyone can ask for. They are one of the many amazing gifts God has given me to show how much He loves me. They are spiritual and practical at the same time. PSFA always says:

"Thankfulness is an attitude and state of mind. Those who have a good attitude always rise to a higher altitude and get

more latitude."

I love this because it's so true. I see it everywhere - at work, with my team and superiors; at home with my family members; within my friendship circle; even with strangers. Everyone wants to be appreciated. Beauty is deeper than how you look on the outside. Being someone who rewards others with a heartfelt thank you, even for the smallest task, makes you radiant. Add a smile and you become instantly more beautiful.

I believe the secret to David's success (I love me some David) is that he praised God at every turn. His words of praise are simply beautiful to read (just go through the Psalms).   To be beautiful you need to fill your mouth with praise and thankfulness.   Who doesn't like being complimented or uplifted?   Have you ever seen a jeweller taking care of his gems or a newly engaged woman caring for her ring? She praises it constantly. Praise is shown in the way the jewel is polished and diligently tended to. We all know people who seem to moan and complain all the time - they drain you of your energy and you would hesitate before spending time with them. But when you are around someone who is grateful and thankful, you literally bask in their presence and time seems to fly by.   As a rare gem, you are supposed to adorn the crown of kings and bring joy to all those who see you. A key aspect of that is thankfulness. It doesn't mean being a doormat - it means being an encourager. Someone who sees the glass as half full, not half empty. Someone who is intent on bringing her own unique flavour to the world.

You cannot be all these things though if you haven't prayerfully learnt to trust and surrender. If you are still trying to control the outcome of things around you, you will be left frustrated, constantly worrying or anxious, dulled to the voice of the Holy Spirit and focused only on the negative. Focusing on negative things or things that don't seem to be going your way does nothing but dullen your shine/radiance and add more wrinkles to your face. No problem has been solved because we focused on all the things going wrong. When you complain or dwell on things that are beyond your control, you feel hopeless and you make bad decisions.

The Bible is so clear about the outcome of grumbling or complaining: it leads only to destruction (1 Corinthians 10:10 NKJV). When I find myself slipping into negative thought patterns, I have to walk myself back by focusing on all the good things in my life. When I struggle with that, I start thanking God (the Psalms really help me here). I love how raw and real David is with God. He's screaming at God for neglecting him and in the same breath singing his praises and adoring him (Psalm 6:1-9, 10: 12-14 as examples). I do the same - I love the scriptures for this reason. Reading the scriptures, I no longer feel alone in my angst, and my grumbling turns to praise.

Determine what doing you looks like - not just saying this is me and staying as God found you (in the dirt of indecision, suffering, pain, gossip, holding grudges, being proud and obnoxious) - but the growth and evolution God is working out in you through his Spirit. How do you separate yourself from all the synthetic versions masquerading as vault items out there? Gemstones like sapphires are often heat-treated to improve their colour and that treatment is permanent. In the fire of the Holy Spirit, you should also be on the lookout for how God wants to treat you so your colour and shine is improved. Rick Warren said it this way, "God changes caterpillars into butterflies, sands into pearls and coal into diamonds using time and pressure. He's working on you too."

The thing to do now is rest and say to our Father, "What's next Papa?" (Romans 8:15-17). What do you want me to change? What do you want me to do with the gifts you have deposited inside me? What is the purpose you want to fulfill in me? Who am I to serve? Scream out to God like David did and ask Him to give you a job teaching rebels His ways so the lost can find their way home – in the same way you found your way home. God is after true change from the inside out; to conceive a new life in you. (Psalm 51:13) It's time to start experiencing life on God's terms.

11

ANYTHING YOUR HAND FINDS TO DO

You were put on this earth for a purpose. You wouldn't be alive if there weren't something amazing still in your future
Billy Cox

Experiencing life on God's terms involves prayerfully exploring and discovering the purpose God has for you. When the going gets tough, you need to know what God's purpose for you is, if you don't want to give up and relegate yourself to being MT.

I have always thought I didn't have any gifts - none of worth to others, anyway. All I could do seemed to be intangible, airy-fairy things. I like to be with people and make people feel better about themselves. I like to connect people, and I like to help people figure out their next move. I'm a doer and a fixer who doesn't mind getting her hands dirty. One of my biggest weaknesses is overcommitting myself because I often forget my own limitations.

I am not a dreamer, though, and I have never thought of myself as the "ideas person" but I enjoy being around dreamers. I love to help people execute their big, seemingly impossible plans. Even as the dreamer is concocting their plan, my mind is rushing ahead to the potential impact of their ideas and I see the pieces even they can't see yet. I really get a buzz from this, and that buzz stays with me until that idea becomes a reality. What I've come to realise, is that my role as an executor is actually vital and important. Every dreamer needs someone practical and full of the right energy who can grasp their vision if he or she wants to actually manifest that idea in the world.

"We won't be distracted by comparison if we are captivated by purpose"
Bob Goff

I've come to realise that all those airy-fairy abilities I have, are actually really important. One day I came across an article on Desiree Rogers (former White House Social Secretary under the Obama Administration). She is a high profile, stylish, businesswoman with an amazing social network, which she channelled to help the Obamas into the White

House. The idea that someone could use something as airy-fairy as her social connections to such tremendous impact made my heart leap for joy. It was the first time that I had ever associated any value with something that came naturally to me. I am a people person and find that I tend to be a connector. I had never placed any value on it before but suddenly I started looking at my ability to connect easily with people as an asset. I like her style, her candid approach to politics, and her social flare but most importantly, I liked that she presented me with a different lens with which to view myself.

This is just one of many occasions where I recognised the tremendously diverse gifts God has given each of us. We can't all be social butterflies or dreamers or introverts. What use would it be if we were all the same? Of what use would the variants in the gems be? We are meant to be of practical use in God's hands so our diversity is what makes us useful. Even in the human body, there is a need for every single body part. We can't all be necks, or belly buttons - how would we get anywhere? Every part has its role to play and none is more important than the other. Together, they make the body function. I love how the scripture puts it in1 Corinthians 12:19-24.

"An enormous eye or a gigantic hand wouldn't be a body, but a monster. What we have is one body with many parts, each its proper size and in its proper place. No part is important on its own."

The important part is that you are using everything in your arsenal of gifts and talents to glorify God - thereby fulfilling his purpose. If you haven't figured out what you have, start in service and pray for God to reveal to you what you are meant to be doing in that particular season. It could be while serving as a host or in hospitality in your local church community that you discover your hidden treasure.

The scripture in Daniel speaks about looking after the needs of the down-and-out. Different Bible versions describe the same verse as being kind to the oppressed (NIV) or showing mercy to the poor (NASB). You could look to ways to give of yourself (your time, your energy, your ideas and your resources) to those that need you. It could be little children who need a big sister/brother to show them they are beautiful as they are. It could be young analysts in your company who need to feel empowered to achieve their ambitions and navigate the career ladder. It could be young people who need someone to believe and guide them as they develop into adults. Whatever it is you find to do - just get doing. God will honour that and start building a picture for you of what you are called to do.

"Stay ready – God has a sense of humour!"
Tolu Adesina

I find that God has a sense of humour though, so be prepared for some interesting experiences along the way. Sometimes it is in the things that get you riled up or pull at your heart's strings that you find your true purpose. My sensitive nature and my constant search for acceptance have led to me recognising and wanting to fill what I feel is a compassion gap wherever I spot it. I am willing to expose myself and share my shortcomings in order to help others not fall into the same trap.

The way I choose to be practical in God's hands is to get out there using any medium I can to show his heart and mind to the world. You can do it too. Find something to do and let God teach you how to be his ears, hands, feet, mouth, stomach and everything in between. You have a part to play in His body and in building His house.

Functioning as you should will make you a worthy investment and will eliminate anyone that is not going to help propel and enable you towards achieving and being all you were made to be. No random person can then easily take you out of your spot because you know fully who you are and what you are made to do so they must complement you or keep walking. You won't spend time crying over every random that walks by because you are aware that you are not made to fit in everyone's space. Your spot is specially crafted in a King's crown and together, you will shine brightly for all to admire.

12

THE KING

She is clothed in strength and dignity and she laughs without fear of the future
Proverbs 31:25

Over the past few chapters, I have focused on what it takes to transition into a crown jewel—a jewel worthy of admiration and showcasing. One who has turned trauma into triumph. One who is at rest in their Father's love and purpose. It is only right that as you complete this transition, the focus turns to the king with whom you will shine.

I have spent plenty of time complaining to God about not having had someone in my life as I went on my journey of discovery. Now, after He showed me the value of being hidden and restored, He turned my attention to the qualities I should be prayerfully petitioning for. Let me explain.

One evening, I was alone in my flat watching an episode of "Grey's Anatomy." It was a standard evening, and I was curled up on my sofa enjoying some me time. Then suddenly I heard the Holy Spirit ask me what I wanted in a man. I paused. Surely, He already knew? Why was He asking me a question He already had the answer to?

I tried to keep watching, but the prompting was so strong that I couldn't concentrate on the show. I turned it off and in the silence of my flat that evening, I decided to say out loud what I wanted. I started off with fine and tall and carried on listing physical attributes playfully. Then I felt the Holy Spirit say, "I'm serious – tell me everything." I got very still in that moment.

Don't get me wrong. I want all the physical attributes I mentioned. But I wasn't taking the whole thing seriously. I was just scratching the surface. In that moment though, I chose to speak out loud my pain and fears and told the Holy Spirit that I did not want to play this game if it would bear no fruit. It was like the floodgates opened. I relived all my past experiences where I had been hurt by men I gave everything to, all the times I tried to do things right but the relationship ended anyway. I was on my sofa wailing.

Then suddenly I felt peace. I can't explain it other than to say I poured myself out that day holding nothing back. Afterwards, I decided to say all I wanted. I want a man who is generous with his time, money, energy, love, affection and more—generous with all his resources. I want a man who is kind and compassionate. I want a man who is gracious and forgiving and always willing to give me the benefit of the doubt. I want a man who will fight for us and never give up. I want a man who will not see every door as an exit but once in, would stay in. I want a man who is proud of me and wants to see me win. I want a man who will not only support my dreams, but would share his dreams with me. I want a man who would see me as his confidante and allow me to be his biggest cheerleader. The list went on. Once I started I could not stop.

I would have gone on for another day, but exhaustion caught up with me and I finally stopped speaking and started praying. The Bible says that when we do not have words, our groanings becomes our prayers and the Holy Spirit is there translating and working it out for us. Romans 8:26-28 says this:

"He does our praying in and for us, making prayer out of our wordless sighs, our aching groans. He knows us far better than we know ourselves, knows our pregnant condition, and keeps us present before God. That's why we can be so sure that every detail in our lives of love for God is worked into something good."

I fell asleep feeling so thankful that night. I knew I had had a spiritual encounter and could be at rest knowing that God's got me. I met men after that night that have turned out to be goats and frogs and hyenas but that hasn't discouraged me because I know He heard me and is working my life into something amazing. One of my friends put it this way, using the example of Adam. He said to me that when God said it is not good for man (Adam) to be alone in the book of Genesis, the next thing he did was bring all the animals to parade in front of him. If Adam had thought, "Oh well, God said I shouldn't be alone so surely one of these animals must be my helpmeet," he would have suffered very long and hard indeed. It made me laugh so hard because

I have definitely made that mistake and looked at hyenas dressed in three piece suits thinking surely this is the one (I kid!). What he was saying in essence is, "Rest easy, Tolu – your true mate is coming." Adam didn't see Eve coming. He was put into a deep sleep after finishing the work he had been assigned to do and then tah-dah! Here comes Eve.

God has had to encourage me many times and in many ways since then. But none of them was more encouraging then the story I'm about to relate. I hope this will teach you to start laying your head on God's heart and telling Him what you want but, more importantly, start asking Him about the kind of man He wants for you.

"The promise of God is this: what's ahead of me is always more than what's behind me"
Steven Furtick

One morning, after yet another frog had jumped back into the swamp and left me scratching my head, I went to God and asked what am I doing wrong? In his unique way of dealing with me, He led me to the scripture in Psalm 45 and gave me a very beautiful and personal promise. He took me on a little journey, and this journey has led me to recognise that not every buyer is deserving of a crown jewel. Only a king is worthy.

In the book of Esther, we are introduced to a king who was having trouble keeping his woman's interest. Not because she was a crazy woman, but because she was unfortunately too focused on herself and her own needs to recognise her true worth and holding in his eyes. I once heard PSFA describe it this way: Vashti denied the king access to her because she had a narrow view of her current situation and was too busy doing her own thing to take the time to consider the future or possible future benefits. She didn't want to be inconvenienced and was unavailable physically and emotionally. That hit me.

Often, you don't realise the vibe you are putting out there. Are you putting people off by being emotionally unavailable because you haven't dealt with some of the kinks you are carrying? Are you willing to put someone else's needs over yours? Are you quick to get angry and blow up over the smallest things? Are you willing to support someone else's dreams even if it makes no sense to you? Doing life with another isn't easy. Think about the fact that there are no perfect people so therefore, even the king will also have his own hang-ups.

Outside of Vashti's reactions however, I was particularly drawn to the king's behaviour and attributes, and I want to focus on some of those. Remember that God has the hearts of kings in his hand and turns them whichever way He wants. As long as I am intentional in my prayer as directed by the Holy Spirit, I can rest in my understanding that God the Father is working out things for my good. Reading through Esther 1 and 2, these were the key points I saw as necessary prayer points focused on characteristics needed in a King looking for a vault gem. These are:

● He has godly counsellors.

- He is accountable and teachable

- He has a heart after God

- He is surrounded by the right type of women.

- He is willing to compromise and not just stuck on having his own way

- He recognises your value when he sees it

- He is willing to sell all (give things up) to get and keep the vault gem

- He is not intimidated by a woman fulfilling her purpose, but instead wants to compliment and care for her.

These attributes were key in bringing Esther to the presence of the king. Without the multitude of counsellors the king was accustomed to seeking advice from, Vashti would still be throwing her own parties and refusing the king's requests. Esther would still be stuck in Mordecai's house and the Jews would have been eradicated. Instead, due to the king's practice of seeking counsel (Esther 1:12-15), access to the palace was made possible for Esther. Vashti's issue is that she didn't have good, wise counsel around to guide her when she needed it. It is very key to pray specifically about the people that are currently speaking into your man's life and heart. Proverbs 11:14 put it this way:

"The more wise counsel you follow, the better your chances."

The second area to pray on is for a man who is accountable and teachable. As the king, he doesn't have to listen to his counsellors. He can override them at any time. But the king chose to be accountable and teachable and he was agreeable to the words of his advisors (Esther 1:19-20). Thinking practically, if your man weren't someone under authority (to God and to a father/mentor), then when you encounter challenges, there would be no one to help mediate that he will listen to. This is a very precarious situation to find yourself in and would put strain on your relationship.

The prayer is that your man would be accountable, teachable, and a man after God's heart. Like David and Joseph, I am looking for a man who considers God before he acts. The reason Joseph did not sleep with Potiphar's wife was not because he couldn't, but because he was afraid to sin against God. That is the type of man I want. I want a man who is first answerable to God before me. That is the only way I can fully trust him, because I know God wants good and not evil for me. If the king is following God's way in all things, we are assured a sweeter union.

After the King's anger had subsided against Vashti in Esther 2, we see a man who is forgiving. We see him having second thoughts. At that point, his advisers stepped in and started making plans based on the original decree. This is really interesting to me. In my mind, as a king, he should have the final say. Now that he is having second thoughts, surely when they come to him to get the ball rolling on finding a new wife, he could just overrule them. Instead, he wasn't focused on having his own way and he chose to keep following the guidance of his counsel. My prayer is that my (and your) king is open and accountable. He should know when to compromise and follow the guidance and leading of those around him. He should be obedient and a man of his word.

Now we have a King worthy of you. As he approaches the vault, my prayer is that he recognises the value of the gems hidden there. Like the buyer in Matthew 13:45-46, the king is on the hunt for an excellent pearl and he is able to spot the treasure in Esther. My prayer for the King that is coming for our hearts is that he has the following:

- Resources

  He needs to be able to handle the treasure. The rarest of treasures does not come without work. No one is a finished product – even the vault item. If it is grace he needs to handle your past, then pray for a man who is gracious. If it is patience or tenacity, pray those things into his life.

- Vision

  He needs to be far-sighted enough to be willing to sacrifice now for the longer-term reward.

- Fortitude

  He won't be swayed by the FOH/MT stones. Instead, he must be willing to look for the treasure hidden in God's field (read vault) and not get discouraged by the work that might be needed.

Finally, as God showcases us and our king spots us, it is important that we follow the leading of the Holy Spirit. Just as Esther went before the King with nothing other than what Hegai told her to take (Esther 2:15), so should we be in our dealings with the king. The Holy Spirit is the one who would show us what to say or do or bring in order to get noticed and win his admiration. The Holy Spirit will mould our attitudes and behaviours and make us wise and attractive. My prayer then is that, when the king spots us, he will recognise the value we hold and can bring to him. I truly believe my husband would be a king who adores me in the way the king adored Esther (Esther 2:17-18). God's hope for his sons and daughters is that we are always safely in His embrace and that those around us are mirroring His love for us. As for the king, I pray that there will be no veil covering us and he will see us for the vault gems we are and are becoming. I pray that he will not be intimidated, but rather be proud to chase, capture, and care for our heart, as we deserve.

TRUST AND SURRENDER

The core of all you are is the true treasure. The foundation of this statement lies in whose you are - your Father. To accept and love yourself you have to grasp the essence of who He is and the love He has for you. He is fully invested in your success and in your life being worthy of admiration. He has skin in this game!

There are so many different points raised throughout this book - from dealing with the loss of a parent to the over-compensating for this absence through romantic relationships. Shaking off pain is not easy or comfortable or fun. Pain, trauma and emotional stress paralyses you. You can even get comfortable in your current state - it's your known entity. Others might not understand it because they are not you but you are allowed to feel angry or sad or devastated. Acknowledge your feelings because they are valid. You might not even believe yet that you are truly loved. You might feel like the things that have happened to you are so terrible that you need healing first before you can trust and surrender. Your anger might be too raw but the only truth I want to leave you with is that God's plan for you doesn't change based on circumstance. Progress involves change and action and that is never comfortable. The pain is as a result of our fallen world but we have a means of redemption and that is through reconnecting with our Father and tapping into

His plan for us - for our fulfilment.

If you don't know what the plan is - start here:

- Love God - then let him then teach you to
  - Love yourself - and inevitably
    - God will make you a jewel that will enrich the life of others.

Your time is now. Your next chapter starts here.

ACKNOWLEDGEMENTS

I would like to thank God for trusting me with His book. I never envisioned I would ever write a book like this as I feel so unqualified but He really is the God who qualifies the called. This book has left me feeling so raw but healed me in so many ways and I am not worthy of such a responsibility but I am humbled to have been called and I am grateful for the grace to obey.

To my mummy - my rock - thank you for always being ready to answer all my questions and for always being willing to patiently learn more about the woman I am. I am strong because of your consistent display of quiet strength and your love which has carried me through many seasons.

To my babies - Myra and Elora - the best nieces anyone can have. You are my daily motivation to improve myself and keep evolving because I want to be someone you can be proud of. Know that you can and will achieve all you set your mind to. You are loved - never ever doubt that - and you are made to dominate. Greatness is in you. Remember God's plan for you is that you will be encouraged in heart and united in love, so that you may have the full riches of complete understanding, in order that you may know the mystery of God, namely, Christ, in whom are hidden all the treasures of wisdom and knowledge. (Colossians 2:2-3 NIV) Aunty loves you more than anything in this world.

To my amazing PB. Words fail me over and over when it comes to expressing my love and appreciation of you. I don't know what, who or where I would be if you hadn't opened up your doors to me 16 years ago. You are a true mother, sister, mentor, and everything in between - my gift from God. Thank you for encouraging me every step of the way with this book and for always being willing to lend a listening ear and an open heart. You were the first person I shared this vision with and it was your encouragement that allowed me to trust the journey. Thank you a million times over. I love you.

To Pastor Sols - you have shown me dimensions of a father's

love I never thought possible. You uplift, encourage, correct, love, give your unique insight, spend time and much more - all while making me feel completely accepted and loved. I never want to disappoint you and I am so thankful for the gracious way you handle and accept me. You are never too busy to listen to my many crush stories, read drafts of my first book, call and check in on me and you let me be me through it all. Your openness with me and your willingness to drop everything for me EVERY SINGLE TIME is not lost on me. Only God can reward you but I want you to know you are so very loved.

Lastly to my WFTD/WoWaS sisters. My life would be empty without you. Your constant prayers, words of inspiration and motivation, covering, banter, and everything in between makes my life rich! Particularly to my Lollipop, Damy with a Y and Sabine my book mentor - THANK YOU! I have no words to tell you how much you mean to me but we have the rest of our lives for me to show you. You are queens and the world is not ready. Funmi, Abi, Tosin and Toks - you inspire me daily with your strength, love and unique abilities. May we soar higher together and achieve all God has called us to as we build His house.

To my team of helpers, readers, cheerleaders and creative directors - thank you! I have been blessed with an amazing family and so many friends-turned-family. Thank you all for being a part of my journey. Your love has contributed in some way into who I am today. Thank you.

ABOUT THE AUTHOR

Tolu Adesina's true passion is in working with young people to achieve their potential and develop their passion. She is an avid volunteer which led to her co-founding the Women of the Word and Seed Foundation and she spends a majority of her time engaging with teenagers and young adults on issues such as career development, emotional trauma and self-acceptance. She is also active in her local church community and currently sits as the lead of the youth ministry. She enjoys travelling and has visited 5 continents with aspirations of visiting the last 2 in her lifetime. Her passions span from spending quality time with family and friends to exploring and trying new cuisine.

TO CONTACT THE AUTHOR:

www.hiddeninthevault.com

info@hiddeninthevault.com

Social media:

Instagram/Twitter: @tolukekere / @inth3vault

Facebook: In the vault

Made in the USA
Monee, IL
07 July 2026